The Life and Teach

Jillellamudi
Amma

Nancy Chartwell

The Life and Teachings of
Jillellamudi
Amma

EKKIRALA BHARADWAJA

**Editions
INDIA**

An imprint of Stone Hill Foundation Publishing

PUBLISHED FOR THE VISWAJANANI TRUST, HYDERABAD

EDITIONS INDIA
An imprint of STONE HILL FOUNDATION PUBLISHING
G-309, Panampilly Avenue, Panampilly Nagar
Cochin 682036, Kerala, India
editionsindia@asianetindia.com

The Life and Teachings of Jillellamudi Amma
Originally published in 1967 as *Life and Teachings of the Mother*
by Matrusri Publications, Bapatla (A.P.), India
Reissued in this edition in 2007 by Stone Hill Foundation Publishing
ISBN: 81-89658-44-1
Copyright © 2007 by Sree Viswajanani Parishat, Jillellamudi
Sree Viswajanani Parishat, Jillellamudi 522113
Guntur District, Andhra Pradesh, India
Tel.: +91 08643 2273 24
E-mail: svjp.amma@gmail.com
Website: www.viswajanani.org

Cover design by Girija Nair

Printed in India by Maptho Printings, Cochin
Printed on acid-free, partially recycled paper

This limited edition, published on behalf of Viswajanani Trust by
Stone Hill Foundation Publishing under the Editions India
imprint, is for sale in the territory of India only.

Foreword

As part of the wish Amma granted to the Viswajanani Trust, Hyderabad, namely, the publication of literature on Amma, out-of-print books are being reissued. It has taken up to now to reissue this book under the title *The Life and Teachings of Jillellamudi Amma*, following the reprinting of *Talks with Amma* by Rodney Alexander Arms in 2006. This book was originally published as *The Life and Teachings of Mother* by E. Bharadwaja, and is the first authentic version in English of Amma's life, published nearly four decades ago (in 1967 to be precise) at Jillellamudi. This book serves well even today as a concise introduction to Matrusri Anasuya Devi, as she is also known, and has guided many a stranger and newcomer to her place. It has evoked deep interest and a great response from many seekers as an authentic glimpse of Divinity in the form of the Mother of All. The interest it generated in the early years of its publication was such that the reviews about the book, quoting Amma's replies to an ardent seeker's queries, led even one electrical engineer from Amsterdam to undertake a journey to the small, remote village of Jillellamudi to be with Amma!

With no copies available even among old-time visitors, and sensing the great response this book had generated, as well as keeping in view that it provided a valuable intro-duction to Amma, the Viswajanani Trust, Hyderabad, thought it fit to have it reissued and thus make it available to a large section of non-Telugu Indian readers and those around the world.

Regarding the tense used in the text of this book, readers need to bear in mind the year in which the book was first published. It is also to be noted that the conditions and events described in this book pertain to the period during which it was written. For example, in respect to the roads and other infrastructure at Jillellamudi, there has been a sea change since then, with a motorable road running directly to Jillellamudi, electric power and telephone facilities be-ing available, drinking water supply now in place, etc.

Extra material in the form of a *Postscript* has been added to this edition of the book for the benefit of the newcomers or visitors to Jillellamudi, dwelling on the various facets of development that this place had undergone over the years following the publication of the first edition. This material also describes the scene newcomers will find in Jillellamudi after Amma left her physical form in 1985.

The Viswajanani Trust, Hyderabad, records its deep sense of gratitude to the revered Professor M. Sivaramkrishna not only for his Introduction to this book but also for his unstinting support and encouragement in all our endeavours, particularly, the publication of literature on Amma.

The Viswajanani Trust also places on record its grateful-
ness for and deep appreciation of the prompt response from
the President, Sree Viswajanani Parishat, Jillellamudi, in
according permission to reissue this book and for readily
agreeing to provide financial support for this project.

We wish to thank Sri P.S.R. Anjaneya Prasad for sparing
the original copy of the book that provided the basis for
bringing out the reissued version, and Srimati Rani Samyukta
for having provided the photograph of the author. We thank
Mr. R.P. Shenoy for making available, free of cost, the pho-
tographs of Amma on a CD to be used in the cover design
of this book.

The Trust is very appreciative of Mr. D.V.N. Kamaraju,
who made a valuable contribution to this project by writ-
ing the Postscript for the book.

Last but not least, we are grateful to brother Tangirala
Kesava Sarma for his constant encouragement and advice
at every step, right from the beginning, and for his interac-
tion with the publisher in bringing about the publication
of this book through him.

VISWAJANANI TRUST
Hyderabad (A.P.)

Publisher's Preface

WE AT STONE HILL FOUNDATION PUBLISHING feel immensely privileged to have been "chosen" to reissue this comprehensive book, which is a valuable record of the life and teachings of Amma Anasuya Devi of Jillellamudi, the Mother of All. To us her teachings are as clear and powerful as those of sages Ramana Maharshi and Nisargadatta Maharaj, and like them, she is a unique manifestation of the Divine. Amma has an added dimension in that she embodied Universal Motherhood, aspects of which directly influenced those who came into contact with her, giving them an intimate sharing of motherly care and compassion.

Our contact with the representatives of the organizations that carry on Amma's work came about when we granted translation and serialization rights to the Viswajanani Trust for the chapter "Anasuya Devi" in Timothy Conway's *Women of Power and Grace: Nine Astonishing, Inspiring Luminaries of Our Time*. Two brethren, Sri Tangirala Kesava Sarma and Dr. Simhadri Sastry Tangirala, very ably negotiated the publishing contract with us for reissuing this book, with gentle persuasion and care. Throughout the publishing process, we felt their guidance and help, which are examples to us of the love and care that Amma's children share.

In reissuing this book, as publishers, we have preserved the unique flavour of the author's language and style, which aptly capture the mood of many a conversation with Amma and the ambience of the Jillellamudi ashram during her time, and shed light on her teachings. The author's use of gender ("he" rather "she") has been retained as it reflects merely the literary choice of the time when this book was written and was in no way meant to convey any feeling of male dominance.

In this book Amma Anasuya Devi of Jillellamudi has been referred to variously as Mother, the Mother, Amma, the Universal Mother, and Mother of All. For the sake of those readers unfamiliar with terms in Sanskrit and other Indian languages, a glossary has been compiled at the end of the text.

The Postscript not only brings readers up to date with events and changes in the Jillellamudi ashram since 1967 but also fills in details the reader will find useful in appreciating Amma's story more fully. Therefore, it has been included at the beginning of the book rather than at the end where a postscript would normally find its place.

Preface to the First Edition

THIS BOOK IS ABOUT Mother [Jillellamudi Amma], written not owing to my pretensions to good authorship but in a spirit of service to my brethren. This fact is the only apology, if one is needed, that can be offered for the faults in the book: faults in expression or in printing.

In Chapter I, the main events of Mother's life are outlined without any attempt to make it a biography.

Chapter II affords glimpses of the institution that is growing around Mother, as the newcomer finds it.

In Chapter III it is my attempt to describe the person of Mother, the general feeling of the visitors [to Jillellamudi], and certain hidden sides of her personality, which I have noted during the four years of my acquaintance with her. The sections of this chapter are reprints from the earlier issues of the English monthly *Matrusri*, in which I tried to introduce Mother to the reader.

In Chapter IV are examples of experiences of the devotees of Mother. They may not be typical but are just what could be mustered from the reluctance of the devotees to speak about their experiences.

Chapter V illustrates the way conversation *usually* goes on between Mother and her visitors—once again, necessarily an incomplete representation, in view of the very wide range of discussions.

In Chapter VI is a random selection of some of Mother's sayings.

The whole book is intended to serve as a kind of introduction [to Mother] or [as a] visitor's guide, and an attempt has been made to illustrate as many aspects [of these as] possible within the scope of a book of this size.

E. Bharadwaja

Postscript

With a view to apprising the reader of the developments and events in Jillellamudi subsequent to the publication of the first edition of this book, a brief account is presented in the following pages.

HYMALAYAM

Hyma was the only daughter of Amma among her three children, one son being elder and one younger. Her life is a saga of mystery. Even though she was the only daughter of the Divine Mother, her life was never a bed of roses or wrapped in comforts. Ill health was her constant companion. She suffered from frequent spasms of headache, fever, and painful sores in the mouth. Illness was also one of the reasons for her discontinued education after primary schooling; she used to learn Hindi and Sanskrit through private tuitions.

The amazing fact was that, with all this suffering, she never complained, neither did she ever pray to Amma for help. On the contrary, if anybody around her had the smallest pain or suffering, she used to run to Mother, praying for their relief. She never used to rest till their suffering was lessened. A small incident explains the magnitude of her immense compassion and love towards fellow beings and Nature. One day, out of a bird's nest, a few eggs had fallen on the ground, and Hyma happened to pass that way. The damage caused to the would-be offspring of the bird upset Hyma so much that she was melancholic and could not take her food that day!

Ekkirala Bharadwaja, the author of this book, lost his mother at the tender age of four. While he was engaged in his spiritual pursuits in the company of Mother at Jillellamudi, the fact that he was denied maternal love at a young age used to haunt Hyma so much that she developed an overpowering maternal love for him, though she was younger to him in age. She wanted to nurse him like a mother and compensate for all the love and care that he missed in his childhood. She used to assert that this was not out of pity for him but to satisfy the growing unrest of her inner self.

Hyma's short life of 25 years was spent only in caring for others rather than herself. Her priority was concern for anyone who was unhappy. Her whole mental occupation was thinking about Amma. Hyma was the personification of kindness, having attained the pinnacle of devotion. If the qualities of selfless service, compassion, Grace, and Bliss enable humans to evolve into the Divine, Hyma was made just for that.

As she grew into full womanhood, Amma was urged to find a suitable match for Hyma and settle her marriage. But the Divine Mother had other plans for her. The very creation of Hyma was for the benefit of humanity. Amma used to dodge the proposal, saying that she would consider Hyma's marriage only after her 25th year.

It was at this age that Hyma suffered from an ailment while in Aurangabad in February 1968, which was later diagnosed as smallpox. On her return to Jillellamudi on the 28th of March 1968, she was put on medication, and responded very well, appearing to have recovered. But Amma knew the lurking seriousness of the disease deep inside. It resurfaced on the 1st of April and, by the 5th, took a severe turn for the worse. She was rushed to the Government General Hospital in Guntur in spite of Amma's advice to the contrary. She breathed her last in the evening in her hospital bed, and was immediately brought back to Jillellamudi, to the shock and unabated grief of everyone there.

Hyma was entombed in the evening of the 6th in a pit 30 feet away from the entrance to Amma's hut. Amma personally oversaw the whole process, making her body sit in the yogic posture *siddhasana*. Sitting on the edge of the pit, Amma put her foot on the crown of Hyma's head as a culmination to the process. At the very touch of Amma's foot, blood oozed out of Hyma's head like a fountain. She had shown to everybody's amazement that Hyma's body was warm, with her chest heaving, suggesting that she was breathing. Amma then declared that the temple to be built on the spot where Hyma was consecrated would be a great spiritual centre and the ultimate destination of many a spiritual seeker. This temple is now called Hymalayam.

After leaving the physical plane, Hyma's kindness and compassion to humanity has been found to be more pronounced and profound. It is the experience of many devotees that the prayers sought from her are instantly answered.

After Hymalayam came into existence, Amma moved her residence to the House of All where she stayed till she left her body in 1985. She never gave open discourses or propounded theories and practices. Amma strongly advocated oneness of the universe despite its appearing diverse. "One has become many" is the secret of this creation, and that One is none other than herself.

Amma, for the first time since 1962, moved out of Jillellamudi, touring a number of places, granting darshan to millions of people. She first visited Mahaboobabad and Warangal in 1973. She was in Hyderabad for about 22 days in April 1974, when she visited several slums (around 65), hospitals, jails, leper homes, and homes for the aged, disabled, and destitute, apart from granting public darshan at different college grounds. She made a special trip to Hyderabad once again in October 1974 to visit one of her first foreign devotees, J.F. Nieland of Holland, who had just recovered from a near-death situation.

GOLDEN JUBILEE

As she was born on Wednesday, the 28th of March 1923, Amma would have completed 50 years in this world in 1973. It was a significant occasion for the devotee children at large, and they wanted to make it a most memorable event. After prolonged discussion they could not come to any conclusion on what should be done to make it so. Somebody suggested that a purse of Rupees 1 lakh be presented to Amma. (One lakh rupees was a huge sum 35 years back.) When this proposal was put before Amma, she reacted immediately, saying that she would be happy seeing one lakh of her children taking food together on that day rather than being presented with a purse of that amount. This triggered action among her devotee children, but the challenge or task before them was not an ordinary one. Even if they were prepared to feed one lakh people, where to find that many in the remote hamlet of Jillellamudi?

Nonetheless, arrangements were made, and a sumptuous menu devised to feed this number was ready by the morning of April 12, Amma's Golden Jubilee birthday as per the lunar calendar. The sceptics among the organizers were not sure that one lakh people would really gather to take food on that day. So food was actually prepared for about 70 to 75 thousand people only. True to their doubts, till 9:30 in the morning on that day, hardly two or three thousand people were present, to the utter disappointment of the organizers. But the next two hours changed the whole scenario at Jillellamudi. Crowds started swarming the place, arriving by all sorts of transport, and by midday the number exceeded all expectations.

The organizers of the feast were again in a dilemma for obvious reasons. Amma's personal aide and Secretary of her organization, Sri Kondamudi Ramakrishna, approached Amma with the predicament before him. Amma smiled at him and said, "You can't start cooking all over now anyway! You go ahead with your own arrangements .... Let me take a bath." It was indeed an implied assurance from Amma!

What was witnessed on that day was truly a miracle that remains unparalleled in history. More than one-and-a-half lakh people received Amma's *prasadam* as lunch on that day. No logic can explain how food prepared for 70 to 75 thousand people was sufficient for that many more. It was a magnificent sight to behold and, besides, even reptiles, insects, and aquatic creatures partook of the prasadam when the food that remained was sprinkled over the fields and poured into the nearby river at Amma's suggestion.

All this triggered speculation among sceptics that the institution that had grown up around her was endowed with a large amount of funds, and that Amma had accumulated enormous wealth. The facts were entirely to the contrary.

However, in December 1975, Naxalites, an extremist group of Communists, attacked the institution with the intention of killing Amma and carrying away the treasure they presumed to be lying with her. They failed on both counts. No doubt that Amma had a treasure in her possession—but it was not a treasure of material wealth. It was a treasure of unbounded love, compassion, and unparalleled forbearance. The Naxalites wanted to kill Amma who, they presumed, was exploiting the poor and the gullible. They encountered resistance from an unexpected source in the form of K.B.G. Krishna Murthy who stood between Amma and the extremists. He tried to reason with them and finally dared them to kill him first before laying their hands on Amma. Blind dogmatism sees no reasoning. They hit him hard, but their blows were received by Amma in the form of the rings he wore bearing Amma's images. They snatched the rings and ran away. Krishna Murthy was badly hurt but recovered fast.

Shortly thereafter, some of the attackers were arrested and brought before Amma for identification. The shepherd never loses count of the sheep, and Mother never fails to recognise her children. Amma identified them only as Her children and not as attackers. She instructed that they be treated with love, and food cooked in Annapurnalayam be served to them with the due regard that is bestowed on others. She even presented them with clothes and saw them off without pressing any charges!

The coastal parts of Krishna and Guntur districts were the targets of a devastating cyclone on the 19th of November, 1977. Being close to the coast, Jillellamudi also suffered the fury of the cyclone, with flood waters engulfing the whole area around the main building of the institution. Power lines and telephone poles were uprooted. The population of the entire village and the inmates of the institution took shelter in the building, and Amma instructed that food be prepared and served to everyone there. When the fury of the cyclone abated after two or three days, Amma, along with Nannagaru and several others, undertook a trip to Diviseema in Krishna District, which was the worst hit. Food packets, blankets, towels, and clothes were distributed to all those in distress. Here, again, food packets, blankets, and clothes were brought in limited numbers. Eyewitnesses still vouchsafe that the distribution through Amma's hands went on unabated throughout the day, surpassing the number of items actually brought there. Amma went close to many of the affected people, hugging and consoling them.

AMMA'S ILL HEALTH

Amma never enjoyed perfect health during her entire life. The irony is that she never had good health but she was never sickly in appearance or conduct. Even in her childhood, some ailment or other was constantly afflicting her.

When she was only four or five years old, she visited her maternal aunt Bhagyamma at Nambur in Guntur District. While in Nambur, she became sick with measles and high fever. Though the effect of measles came down in four to five days, high fever continued for nearly two months with most painful mouth sores, sore throat, etc. After two-and-a-half months of suffering, her maternal aunt and uncle decided to send her back to her father. In spite of such prolonged sickness, all the villagers who came to see her off were surprised to see the brightness and radiating glow on her face. After reaching her grandfather's house in Bapatla, the treatment continued for more than one-and-a-half months.

IT WAS THE 17TH of July 1975. Amma had been suffering with a big abscess on her thigh for the last four months. While she was bearing the pain silently, it was simply unbearable for the devotee children around her. Amma was constantly lying on the cot. Even a small movement from one side to the other was very painful. An emergency call was sent to Dr. S.V. Subba Rao of Nellore, Dr. Kesava Rao of Narsapuram, and Dr. (Mrs.) Janaki Devi of Madanapalle, who promptly came to treat her. Treatment was started but the response was not encouraging. July 19 was a festive day (*tholi ekadasi*), and nearly 400 devotees from different places gathered to have darshan of Amma. Amma's compassion knows no bounds—even in that condition, she came out

of the room to give darshan to the devotees, sitting on a
sofa for nearly four hours without a trace of pain on her
radiant countenance!

However, by that night the abscess had become worse in
size, and the doctors decided that surgery was inevitable.
Amma had to be moved to a nursing home where all the
facilities were available to perform the operation. But to
move Amma from the second floor was a daunting task as
she was not in a position to move. A few offered to lift Amma
to the car on the ground floor. Amma did not support the
proposal as the people around might be upset by the sight.
At last, she herself suggested the solution. Let the doctors
cut the abscess so that she could walk. The doctors did not
foresee this event as they did not bring the required instruments. Again, Amma herself suggested the solution. She
advised that a sterilized razor blade might be used for cut-
ting the abscess! *What a cruel and primitive way of treating
the Divine Mother!* But, the doctors had no option! Finally,
repeatedly encouraged by Amma, Dr. S.V. Subba Rao performed the operation in her room where neither electricity
nor any anaesthesia was available. After an hour's rest,
Amma came down the stairs to proceed to Nellore for further treatment.

The Divine play is incomprehensible! When the suffering of human beings exceeds tolerable limits, the Supreme
cannot remain a dispassionate observer. A cry for help cannot go unanswered. The suffering is instantly accepted by

the Divine in human form and is taken on her person. Here, the primordial energy has assumed a human form in flesh and blood. But that body cannot be equated with any other human body as no ordinary human can withstand the trials and tribulations that Amma was subjected to.

Towards the end of August 1980, Amma's health appeared to take a serious turn, with Amma struggling to breathe. Immediately, Dr. S.V. Subba Rao was informed on the phone and summoned, while the doctors attending on her continued their efforts. On arrival, Dr. Subba Rao commenced treatment, taking note of the fact that Amma had been a diabetic since 1968 with an enlarged heart since 1975, accompanied by high blood pressure. He diagnosed the disease as pleurisy because of pneumonia. After Amma showed improvement in her condition, he left for Nellore.

As a follow up, x-rays were taken of Amma's chest and sent to Dr. Subba Rao, who saw a lump in one of Amma's lungs and advised that Amma be taken either to Madras or Hyderabad for diagnosis and further treatment. Accordingly, she was taken to Hyderabad in October 1980, where she stayed in devotee Rajagopalachary's house. Doctors of different specialties visited and examined her at the place of her residence and commenced treatment. The verdict and diagnoses of the doctors were as varied as their branches of specialties! At one stage, they even speculated that Mother was afflicted with cancer.

After a month-long treatment, Dr. Rajagopalan, a famous cardiologist who was also part of the team that treated her, finally declared on November 1—to the extreme happiness and joy of one and all—that Amma was completely cured.

After making visits to houses of the devotees, Amma, along with her entourage, left on November 13 by train to Bapatla.

DEMISE OF NANNAGARU

During the early hours of the 16th of February 1981, Nannagaru (Amma's husband), sleeping on the ground floor of her quarters, had a sudden and massive heart attack, to which he succumbed. When one of the inmates rushed to Amma to convey this news, she instructed that he be brought upstairs immediately. A cot was placed beside Amma's where he was laid. Amma, moving close to Nannagaru's cot, and turning towards him, put her hand on his chest, and they remained like that for the whole day.

Anxious and grieving villagers thronged the place, and with no sign of Amma getting up, they filed in a queue inside the room one after the other and did pranams to Amma and Nannagaru, touching their feet.

Amma got up in the night. She then said Nannagaru would be interred in the main temple and suggested that necessary arrangements be made. On the morning of the 17th, many of the relatives and devotees who received the sad news arrived in Jillellamudi. Amma arrived at Hymalayam at noon, and the devotees from Visakhapatnam did

puja to her with Lalita Sahasranamam while Amma sat on
the dais arranged in front of Hymalayam.

In the meantime, Nannagaru's body was brought and,
as per Amma's instructions, it was kept leaning on the
Hymalayam wall. Amidst chanting of mantras by the Veda
pundits, Amma gave an oil bath to Nannagaru, and did *abhishekam* with milk and later with water. After everyone who
gathered there did abhishekam with milk, she once again
did abhishekam with *panchamritas* and with water. Amma
smeared various perfumes all over his body and put new
clothes on him. She applied vibhuti and kumkum (vermil-
lion) on his forehead in the Shaiva and Vaishnava traditions,
and put on him a new *yagnopaveetam*. She draped his body
with a silk saree that she wore earlier, put garlands around
his neck, and showered flowers of various hues over him.

Many of those around noticed blood oozing out of his
nostrils as Amma was performing abhishekam to him, a sight
akin to what happened to Hyma when she was being interred. Another strange aspect was that the body remained
as it was 24 hours ago even though no steps for preserving
it were taken, except for Amma's hand resting over his chest.

Around 3 p.m. Amma entered the sanctum of the temple
along with Nannagaru's body and, to the accompaniment of
chanting of *Sri Suktam*, *Purusha Suktam*, and *Prithvi Suktam*,
the body was made to sit in *padmasana* in the pit prepared
on the right side as we face the temple entrance. She poured
salt and vibhuti powder all over his body, almost drowning

him in them. She removed the gold rings on her fingers and toes, gold bangles, and nose stud, and threw them in the pit. She offered even the saree and blouse she was wearing till then, changing into new clothes and wearing another set of ornaments to the satisfaction of everybody.

Amma later named the temple Anasuyeswaralayam. On the morning of the 18th she personally lit the traditional lamp and initiated daily worship in the temple.

UNIVERSAL COMPASSION

The 5th of May 1984 remains in the memory of everyone in Jillellamudi who happened to witness a momentous occasion. Married on the 5th of May 1936, it was the 48th wedding anniversary of Amma, and naturally had special significance in Jillellamudi. Ever since laying the foundation stone for the temple on this day in 1956, Amma had performed some activity or the other connected with the temple every year, apart from performing the weddings of several of the devotees, including her own two sons. She used to climb over the top of the temple and perform sanctifying rituals year after year on May 5. However, she stopped this practice after Nannagaru was consecrated in the temple sanctorum in 1981; she would only break coconuts going round the temple. Amma stopped doing even this after May 1983.

The 5th of May 1984 assumed special significance because of the way Amma demonstrated her unbounded love for every being. She had instructed earlier that all the villagers be assembled in the ashram premises in the evening and, similarly, all types of cattle in the village be brought there on the morning of the 6th.

Accordingly, all the villagers assembled there in the evening of May 5, when Amma arrived and sat on the dais. The young ladies among the inmates applied wet turmeric powder to the feet, sandal paste to the necks, and kumkum marks on the foreheads of the womenfolk, and distributed bangles among them as per Amma's instructions. Then, as the names of members of each family were being called, each one of them came on to the dais and received new clothes from Amma. Following Amma's instructions, all of them returned to her wearing the new clothes. They were then served food, which they partook to their heart's content.

The next day, all types of cattle, including cows and buffaloes, and goats and sheep in the village were brought there in the morning. They were all fed with cattle feed specially brought from Sangamjagarlamudi, a place famous for its dairy industry.

JOURNEY INTO ETERNITY

The first half of 1985 marked a glorious saga of events in Jillellamudi. As if preparing for her journey into Eternity, Amma designed several events, the great merriment over which made the residents and other devotees there fully engrossed, and which caught them unawares in the end. From the 22nd of January 1985, Amma stayed for about 40 days in Ravi's (Amma's second son) house in Jillellamudi, where he lived by virtue of his posting in the branch of the State Bank of India there. Each of these 40 days was like a festival with several programmes arranged during that period. It was at this time that she visited the houses of staff members of the Oriental College, workers serving the institution, and houses of devotees who had settled in Jillellamudi. There was a grand celebration of Amma's birthday in April, and her wedding day on May 5.

During the first week of June 1985, Amma's health suddenly took a serious turn and gradually worsened. The team of doctors attending on her did their best while praying to Amma to cure herself. But the Divine Will prevailed, and Amma shed her mortal body in the night of the 12th of June 1985, thus bringing the curtain down on an era of unlimited power manifesting in her limited physical form. Amma continues to demonstrate her presence through innumerable experiences of the devotees, both through her voice to some and answering the distress calls of others.

Introduction

THE DIVINE PLAY OF THE
GODDESS HERSELF

IS AN INTRODUCTION NEEDED to this book? Plunge into it straight-away and you will find yourself in a Presence that is se-renely staggering, extraordinarily ordinary, and miraculously natural. I use paradoxes deliberately, for this personage and her story hardly conform to logical axioms or the usual hy-perbole of so-called spirituality. What Lakelly-Hunt says about faith and feminism (in the context of poet Emily Dickinson) is the literal truth of Mother's life: "Experience transcendence in the mundane and glory in the paradox."

But, then, why these lines of introduction? They are to share my joy, an abiding sense of what it is to experience, face to face, lived spirituality. Even "spirituality" is a question-begging word. Everything about this Mother of All is so incredibly natural, invariably commonsensical, that, in retrospect, you wonder whether such profound wisdom can be so simple.

Look, for instance, at the role she enacted as an ordinary housewife (which she was) and juxtapose it with the varied perceptions of those who had her *darshan*. Married and taking care of all that involved, she yet revealed herself in an unmistakable way as the incarnation of the Divine. "She was looking after the needs of the family, doing all the domestic work herself—fetching water from the freshwater tank at the end of the village, making dung cakes for fuel, making ropes out of fibre, tending and milking the cattle, receiving the visitors to the family and to the village, etc."

Yet her birth was one of those Self-propelled advents of the Divine (*svayambhu*) that is contingent on temporal, spatial, and causal criteria—so common whenever a divine being enters the shores of the world. Time and the timeless coalesce here; we have the timeless tempered by time—and time redeemed by the timeless. Should one believe all these details of her appearance? The author, Bharadwaja, asks Mother herself. "How should I know?" she responds plainly, then adds, "Come, let us ask my father."

This is typical of the authenticity of this book, the first biography in English of this remarkable Mother. Similarly, the father tells what transpired in a dream he had:

"Who are you?" he asked her in the dream.
"I am the Mother," she replied.
"Whose mother?" he again asked her.
"I am the Mother of All," she replied.

Strange Mother, indeed. As Bharadwaja's narrative shows, Mother unfolds her splendour in serene, subdued phases. These aspects prompt the most nagging questions that have perennially baffled the best brains of humanity. For instance, Ramana Maharshi had the experience of death when he was seventeen years old. And "meditation" on that gave him an awakening to the Ultimate Reality that never left him. And it gave us the most universally practical mode of Self-enquiry based on the "simple" question "Who am I?" Bhagavan Ramana never felt any fear or anything unnatural in that experience. As Jiddu Krishnamurti said, "Only at the point of death many people realize that they have not lived at all!" And at the point of seeming death, Bhagavan entered the immortal life of perennial joy.

Now, juxtapose Mother's exposure. She was four years old when her mother died. Her father, unable to bear the grief, cried, "Your mother is dead and gone forever from us."

"Where has she gone, Father?" she calmly asked him.
"Yes, whither?" he muttered to himself.
"Tell me first of all, whence she came, Father?"
Then she asked him slowly, "What does dying mean?"

To her grandfather, she puts the same question. After a few such questions comes the next natural revelation about the persistence of sorrow. She asks her grandfather:

"Tell me, where do they [the dead] go?"

"To God."

"Why?"

."It is his will."

"If the one who was sent by God were to return to Him at his will, then why should we weep for it?"

The question is a perennial one. Right from Nachiketa of the *Upanishads*, through texts like *Hamlet*, to Jiddu Krishnamurti and beyond, sages and saints put the question and affirm that there is no death at all. But our weeping for the dead, ironically forgetting that we ourselves die and the living weep for us, is the incessant impulse that, perhaps, impels the advent of beings such as Mother, who defy death and live on in the hearts of countless seekers. They are what Sri Ram called them—"sweepers of sorrow," the sorrow that persists in human consciousness.

Thus began the "ministrations" of Mother. Underlying all that she did and spoke was disregard of distinctions and differences so that her all-encompassing love literally engulfed everyone in her fold. The *modus operandi*, it seems to me, is to take ordinary words and concepts and turn them upside down. You are simply startled by what the learned, yet devout, author calls "her intelligence, mental balance, and deep insight." The most remarkable thing is the peculiar and fascinating play on words. These are words that seemingly reflect the *vaikhari* level (the level of verbal meaning and syntax), only to take a quantum leap into the *para l*evel of language (the level at which the word reveals more than what it states).

Everywhere, we find this *chamatkar*. For instance, a respected swami, Kalyanananda Bharathi, asks her:

"Who are you?"

Anasuya: "I came here to know *that* because I do not know who I am."

Swami: "What is your caste?"

Anasuya: "Mine is the caste of *shukla* and *shonita*." [emphasis mine]

One of the most remarkable comments, "I came here to know that," sets up several reflections. "That thou Art" (*tattvamasi*), declared the *Upanishads*. Perhaps, these nuances are lost on the swami. Similarly, the question about caste is somewhat surprising. Does that matter in matters spiritual? "The devotees are all of one caste," declared Sri Ramakrishna. The most staggering is the negation of all caste as Mother points to the universal genetic process of birth as a result of the male and female union. It is a mingling of these two that goes into the making of the child. The act of creation and its processes have no distinctions of class or caste. Isn't it appropriate that the Mother of All should point to the generic, genetic process of universal creation? Does caste matter to her? In spite of being a swami, her questioner is no exception to the innate paradigm of varied perceptions depending on levels of mind and sensibility:

"Tell me of your real identity," the swami cried.
"Reality itself is my state," she coolly replied.
"How do your people view you?" he asked.
"They view me as I appear to them. Mind is the measuring rod. They measure me only according to the range of their mind."
With an abrupt salutation, she took leave of him, and walked out as swiftly and silently as does a vision or a revelation!

This explains why Mother was "suspected of being mentally retarded by some, as being ill by others, as being possessed by a devil by yet others." Indeed, she was admitted to Bayer Hospital at Chirala. But, here, "Mother was so much admired and loved by all the doctors and nurses that theirs was no longer the relationship of doctors, nurses, and a patient ..."

This is no ordinary unhinging of the mind. It is divine madness, which so voluntarily affects the consciousness that an ecstatic feeling called *bhava* possesses the person. In her study of madness of the saints (especially Indian saints), June McDaniel cites the examples of Chaitanya, Sri Ramakrishna, and Haranath. Haranath was called, indeed, Mad

Haranath: *Pagal* Haranath. The classic case is that of Chaitanya Mahaprabhu:

> Chaitanya's symptoms of *bhava* (made him) appear like a mad elephant. His body was a field of sugarcane in which elephants fought, trampling the cane. His state of divine madness affected his mind and body, causing fatigue, and he spoke possessed by *bhava* [June McDaniel, *The Madness of the Saints*; Chicago, Illinois: The University of Chicago Press, 1989; p.36].

But Mother's "hospitalization" has had an epiphanic function. For, "a few of the European doctors looked upon Mother with reverence and awe that is due to Christ and Mary." After all, if she is the Mother of All, denominational differences and theological variations must certainly find validity and corroboration. Hence her getting linked to Christ! One should indeed be grateful for the so-called madness and the subsequent hospitalization! This also explains Mother's assertion: "No one knows my measure; I am the measure of all."

Saints are generally sceptical of the body. Notions of celibacy, etc., are parts of the spectrum of assumptions. But then these are flexible ones. When the author himself had a doubt in this regard, pat came Mother's clarification: "Sensual pleasures are the very matrix of creation, they are the cause of your birth." Elaborating on the implications, Mother said, further:

"Even the animals that move around you in the lonely forests are enough to taunt you with your innate emotions and desires. Certainly the continuous hard work (of devotees), their continuous chanting of the divine name, their faith, their selflessness, their austerely simple lives are far more efficacious instruments of their inner purification than the mere closing of the eyes of one who has none of these aids to save him from his own passions and cravings."

In Hinduism, spiritual insights are rooted in and manifested as psychological (and psychic) experiences. Seen from this perspective, emotions play a vital role in the flowering of innate perfection. The only caution is that this flowering may subsume, but is not identical with, what these days is being called "emotional intelligence" (books by Daniel Goleman, especially *Emotional Intelligence*).

Mother's mention of animals suggests another remarkable facet: dogs and cats always, strangely, lived in harmony around her. She was so extremely fond of them that often we wonder whether she had more affection for them. Of course, in Hindu spiritual symbology, the dog stands for loyalty (e.g., the dog, as the sole sojourner of Dharmaraja's ascent to heaven, as told in the *Mahabharata*), and the cat for total surrender to one's chosen ideal. The *Marjala Nyaya* holds that, like a kitten that is happy wherever its mother cat places it, so should the devotee surrender (cf.: "I have no other refuge than thee," says the sloka from the *Bhagavad Gita*).

When anyone talked of her devotees, Mother used to
say, "I have no *sishyas* [disciples], all are my *sisus* [i.e., chil-
dren]." Here, for me, is an important clue as to why Mother
was passionately fond of feeding children who came to her.
She would insist on their taking food. Indeed, she was the
tangible manifestation, all felt, of Goddess Annapoorna, in
this regard.

One wonders why she insisted on feeding people. One
clue, perhaps, is the *kosha* paradigm of Hinduism. There is
the primary sheath (*kosha*) called "*annamaya kosha*," the food
dimension. One of the definitions of Brahman, the Ultimate
Reality itself, is that it is food. And when food (often prepared by Mother herself) is partaken, it becomes *prasad* and
sets in motion changes in the body. Eventually, *sattvic* food
blessed by Mother results in subtle unfolding of the deeper
spiritual layers of consciousness.

An analogy will further clarify this point. Many visitors
who normally felt a bit uneasy about crying in public used
to burst into tears as soon as they had *darshan* of Mother.
The author asks Mother whether it marks "a rebirth of the
inner being." Mother agrees and explains:

"In fact, that is not sorrow at all. Ordinary sorrow has
a reason for it. But this has none. You call it weeping
only for want of a better word to describe it. It is not
real weeping."

So, it is not mere eating. It is cleansing the psyche of long-accumulated psychic trash, like a blood transfusion replaces impure blood. As Mother says, "Association with the wise will make the mind sink into the Heart. Such association is both mental and physical." That is the difference between food and *prasad*, if one can put it that way. But, of course, regarding weeping, Mother assures us: "*You need not shed tears. I am always there to look after you.*" (Emphasis added.)

In short, this biography makes for entrancing reading and thoughtful absorption. Mother signals the advent of the Divine Feminine as a balance to excesses of patriarchy. She is in the line of the manifestation of Shakti. In our century, India itself saw the advent of what Linda Johnsen called "Daughters of the Goddess." (Linda Johnsen, *Daughters of the Goddess*; St. Paul, Minnesota: Yes International Publishers, 1994). We had the Holy Mother, Sarada Ma of Ramakrishna–Vivekananda, Anandamayi Ma, Sri Ma of Kamakhya, Mata Amritanandamayi Ma, and many others. Above all, all these represent a cosmic balance that sets right the excesses of radical feminism (cf.: Luce Irigaray, *Between East and West*; New York: Columbia University Press, 2002).

One is grateful, therefore, to the Viswajanani Trust, Hyderabad, and Sree Viswajanani Parishat, Jillellamudi, for the reissue of this biography, long out of print. It is, I am sure, an indispensable, lively introduction to the Mother of All.

At the risk of sounding partisan, I would like to add, in conclusion, that Mother is, of course, a daughter of the Goddess. But then she is the Goddess Herself!

May 2, 2007   Prof. M. Sivaramkrishna
Buddha Jayanti   (Former) Chair
Hyderabad   Department of English
                                            Osmania University
                                            Hyderabad (A.P.)

Contents

CHAPTER I

A Short Sketch of Mother's Life

BIRTH

DURING THE MONTH OF Chaitra (March–April) there is, in nature, a new stirring and a new awakening, and, in all homes, a new activity of a cheerful and festive type. The young and the old wake up in the dark hours before dawn and sing songs of awakening to the Sun and to the Divinity that is dormant in all things. Young girls and housewives assemble in some courtyards for worshipping the cow. The morning breeze blows, brushing the ladies who, having bathed in the village tank, offered oblations, and said their morning prayers, carry fresh water to their houses. It was during this month, when the song of the cuckoo, the chatter of the parrot, and the twitter of the sparrow mingled with the incessant ringing of the bells in the temple in the village of Mannava, and when the whole atmosphere vibrated with the deep chant of the Vedas by austere Brahmins of the village, that the holy Mother of Jillellamudi was born on the 28th of March 1923.

Mannava is a small village in Guntur District of Andhra Pradesh, situated on the Guntur–Ponnur Road. The village was founded seven generations earlier by the ancestors of the Mother of Jillellamudi. It prided itself on the orthodoxy, devotion, and scholarship of its Brahmins, and the perfect harmony in which all the communities and castes lived as members of a single family.

In this village of Mannava lived a pious couple, the late Seethapathi, the village officer, and his wife Rangamma. Their house was frequently the scene of cordial get-togethers of their kith and kin.

The ancestors of Rangamma were ardent devotees of Goddess Bala Tripura Sundari and Goddess Raja Rajeswari. The family had three pious and learned spiritual aspirants in its lineage: *saddhvis* Maridamma and Ammayamma, and the late Chalapathi Rao who practised the three paths of *jnana*, *bhakti*, and *karma yoga*, respectively. This triple stream of spiritual yearning seemed, as it were, to have sanctified the lineage and prepared the way for the birth of the divine child in the family. The late Chidambara Rao, a famous lawyer of Bapatla and the grandfather of the holy Mother, used to remark that his granddaughter Anasuya was the synthesis of the jnana of Maridamma, the bhakti of Ammayamma, and the karma yoga of Chalapathi Rao.

Seethapathi and his wife Rangamma lived in perfect harmony and devotion, but what had sorely weighed on their hearts was the loss of as many as five children. Though Seethapathi was not devout by natural inclination, tradition and the hope of having children bound him in devotion to Lord Chennakesava and His consort Lakshmi. Rangamma herself practised severe austerities and worshipped Goddess Bala Tripura Sundari. She prayed not to have nightmares about the death of her children, for whenever she conceived, it was more the fear of an impending disaster that gripped her heart and stifled the flicker of hope rather than joy at the expectation of a child. In course of time, they were blessed with the birth of a son, Sri Raghava Rao by name, who was to become the headman of the village of Mannava. But the months after his birth were naturally moments of uncertainty and fear for the parents. Whenever Seethapathi was alone, he used to brood over the repeated deaths of his children and how callous his Lord had been to his woes, despite his supplications. The gods were probably not as callous as they seemed; for, finally, another child was born to them on the 28th of March 1923, precisely at the *brahma muhurta*, i.e., during the transition from night to morning, which is considered the most auspicious time of the day by the Hindus.

"MOTHER, DID YOUR FATHER or your mother receive any sign of your advent in their family?" I once asked her. When I put that question, I had in mind the dream of Mayadevi before the birth of the Buddha.

"How should I know? Come, let us ask my father," replied Mother, and she led me to Seethapathi who at that time was confined to his bed with paralysis. She repeated my question to him. Then he recounted that one day, while he was sitting under a tamarind tree brooding over his misfortune regarding children, he had a vision in which he saw a girl of five standing before him. Her face was vaguely familiar to him. The girl transfigured herself into the shape of Lord Chennakesava and Goddess Lakshmi whom he worshipped for a long time. Once again, the two forms vanished behind the form of the five-year-old girl. He was greatly surprised by the experience, for he was quite wakeful and yet the vision was clear and did not seem to be a figment of his own imagination. Finally, he explained it away to himself by holding that his constant worship had resulted in this vision.

A few months before Rangamma was again pregnant, Seethapathi said that he had a dream in which he saw that his house was cleared of all its contents. He also saw a middle-aged woman of great beauty seated in a chair in the middle of the house. She wore *kumkum* prominently between her eyebrows.

"Who are you?" he asked her in his dream.

"I am the Mother," she replied.

"Whose mother?" he again asked her.

"I am the Mother of All," she replied.

Next morning, failing to explain away the dream to himself, as he did in the case of his vision, Seethapathi approached a close friend of his, who was also a great scholar, and sought his interpretation of the dream. The pundit told him that the dream signified the birth of a divine child in their family, the manifestation of Goddess Bala Tripura Sundari, and that the form he had seen in his dream was that of the Goddess. Seethapathi, not being of a deeply devotional and religious bent of mind, was not so happy about that; the fear of a calamity seemed to be more real to him than the possible joy ensuing from what he considered to be a superstitious prediction of the pundit. Of course, this was what Seethapathi felt only after hearing the interpretation, though he had felt more strongly about the dream before he met the pundit.

Days and months passed, and the scroll of time unfolded. Again, Rangamma conceived. Seethapathi said that, from the time of conception, Rangamma experienced unspeakable joy and exaltation. She experienced strange visions and moments of unparalleled bliss. The most remarkable of all was the feeling that she carried the whole creation in her womb unimpaired by the finiteness of her own physical frame. Occasionally, she even felt momentary identification with the Infinite. During such an experience, she was found sitting rapt with inward joy, her eyelids not closing even once! She experienced outbursts of joy that caused either profuse flow of tears or uncontrollable laughter. Rangamma was sometimes afraid that her own life might be endangered.

IF THE MYSTERIOUS EXPERIENCES of Seethapathi and Rangamma during her confinement were like the occasional thunder and lightning that traversed the dark clouds of their apprehensions, the moment of Mother's birth was the sudden cloudburst of miraculous experiences that everyone present there had. It was on the Suddha Ekadasi of the month of Chaitra (i.e., in the eleventh quarter in the brighter half of the lunar month of Chaitra) in 1923 that the child was born. The newborn was so quiet at birth that the parents feared that it was stillborn. The nurse who attended on Rangamma had to sound brass vessels loudly to make the child cry. Strangely enough, the exact moment of her birth coincided with a ceremonial function in the village temple: flags were being hoisted, and bells, conches, and other musical instruments were being sounded.

From the moment of the child's birth, everyone in the room, including Rangamma and the maidservant, had divine visions of the Universal Mother.

The newborn child was given its first milk by Kanakamma who was to be her mother-in-law in the future. Because Rangamma had a sentiment that all the children suckled by her would die, it was decided that the child thereafter be suckled by the woman servant, Nagamma by name. The child exhibited strange conditions of health off and on. It became stiff, with its breath suspended, and stayed in that condition, sometimes as long as four days. All this happened without any apparent crisis in the child's health either before or after this "incident."

In this context, it is interesting to note one fact regarding Mother's life. When visitors asked Mother as to when she had attained perfection, she replied that she was ever the same, and that if there was a difference, it was in their understanding of her and not in her being. This answer pinpoints the peculiarity of her life. The profoundly mystical experiences that were felt by several people in her presence at her birth are felt even today by some visitors to Jillellamudi. The free flow of tears and crying that Rangamma had experienced are experienced by them. Mother's body is as tender and delicate even today as it was in her childhood. Not only human beings but animals like dogs and cats, serpents like cobras, and even insects like scorpions display in her presence a strange awareness of her divinity. They shed their mutual violence and live in harmony.

Let us return to our story of Mother's childhood. The child was named on the twenty-seventh day as Anasuya. On that occasion, B. Nageswara Rao was present as a boy of ten years. A few days after the birth of Anasuya, the old women in the household joked about the marriage of the child to the boy Nageswara Rao. It was in fulfilment of those words that Mother insisted on marrying Nageswara Rao when she grew up to be a girl of fourteen!

That Mother was well aware of all that had happened at every moment in her childhood is evident from the fact that, even as recently as two years ago, she recounted the minute details of several conversations that took place immediately after her birth to her mother-in-law Kanakamma. Kanakamma was surprised at Mother's memory and asked her, "Who told you all these? Even I did not remember them till you recalled them to my memory."

Till the thirtieth day after her birth, the child Anasuya grew up under the care of Rangamma and the servant Nagamma. Anasuya's great-grandmother Maridamma used to spend the day in singing mystical songs while putting the child to sleep or waking her up in the morning. When Maridamma was to leave the village of Mannava, she entrusted the child completely to the care of Nagamma. The child was to be suckled and brought up by Nagamma at her own house, taking her to Rangamma for an hour or two every day. It needs no special mention that Nagamma had several unusual experiences with the child. No wonder that Nagamma compared herself happily with the cowherds in whose company Lord Krishna grew up. What surprised Nagamma most was the fact that the child never cried for milk but was willing to be suckled by her whenever Nagamma wanted to do so.

At the end of a year and a half, Nagamma was asked to return the child to Maridamma who arrived at Mannava. Nagamma felt the pangs of separation to be too acute. As though in response to her silent sadness, Anasuya would not keep quiet unless she was taken by Nagamma to the latter's home at least once a day.

When Anasuya was completing her second year, she once sat under a pomegranate tree in *padmasana* and attained a transcendental state in meditation, with her eyes half closed. Everyone mistook her to be having a fit of epilepsy, not noticing the peculiar lotus posture she had assumed. All sorts of pungent liquids were poured in her eyes and nose to make her conscious, but it was in vain. She returned to her normal consciousness in an hour. Similarly, on another occasion, she was seen sitting in a strange posture with her breath suspended and eyes completely turned inside. When someone asked her later as to what she was doing, she replied that she was in *Sambhavi mudra*. Everyone was astounded at these words and deeds from a child of two years.

Once when Rangamma was returning from Tenali to Mannava, an old man in saffron robes met her and told her that her child was the manifestation of God and that she (Rangamma) had no more need to be born again.

Even as a tender child, Anasuya displayed compassion for the poor. She gave them whatever she had with her—clothes, golden bangles, etc.—and when she was questioned about these articles by the elders, she pretended ignorance, which made the elders think that she was robbed. They used to thank their stars that the child was safe.

Once when she was taken by Rangamma from Ponnur in a cart, the child was allowed to get down to answer the call of nature. Sitting at a particular spot, the child Anasuya said, "This place is good, let us stay here."

"There is no house here; how can we stay?" asked Rangamma.

"Is it necessary?" the child asked with a strange smile. "Can little children stay without their mother?" asked Rangamma. "Why not? When you are no more, I will be the Mother," replied Anasuya.

Strangely enough, Rangamma died within two years after this incident. At the spot where the child Anasuya sat at the time of this conversation, there now stands the image of Goddess Bhramaramba in the temple of Sahasra Lingas!

Before her death, Rangamma herself had perceived strange phenomena operating in her child. Once in her third year, Anasuya was laid up with high fever. Rangamma was sorely weeping, fearing a calamity. Then old Maridamma assured her that, owing to the power of a Rajyalakshmi Yantra that was worshipped by all in the village temple of the goddess, the child would soon recover. Immediately, the child got up and corrected her, saying, "That is not Rajyalakshmi Yantra, it is Rajarajeswari Yantra." Later, in the year 1958 when Mother visited Mannava, she showed everyone the yantra to be that of Rajarajeswari.

As a girl Anasuya never asked for food just as she never cried for milk as a baby. She accepted it because she was given it. In fact, she did not digest what was given. It used to go out as it was, in excreta. She was treated by doctors to no avail. Once an old man in saffron robes tied a very poisonous herb around her neck, warning her not to eat it. At first she refused to wear it. When she was forced to wear it, she chewed it up saying that herbs could neither save nor kill anyone destined to be otherwise. The old man left wondering how the child had survived.

Rangamma again became pregnant and was suffering from cough and fever. It was felt that expert treatment was necessary, and so she was taken in a palanquin from Mannava to Bapatla. On the way, while they passed by the temple of Lord Chennakesava, she heard the bells on the *dhvaja sthambha* ringing. The bearers of the palanquin took off their shoes in reverence and offered their salutations from a distance. Rangamma was also looking at the temple with folded hands. Suddenly, she found her child Anasuya standing on the *gopuram* with her hand stretched out in the manner of a mother welcoming her child. Rangamma turned her gaze in surprise at the child sleeping in her lap. She was still quietly sleeping there!

WHAT IS DEATH?

Even when all the fears of the human heart can be allayed, one of them remains, and that is the fear of death. It is the one mystery, the one veil, past which very few can see. It is the last riddle that must be solved before one can attain to Life Eternal. Many great souls had to tread beyond it before they attained to the highest state of perfection. It was the question of the inevitability of death that had transformed

Siddhartha into the Buddha. Sai Baba of Shirdi was dead for three days before he again came back to life. Thakur Harnath was dead for a few hours while serving in Kashmir before a transformation took place in him and he became a gracious saviour. It was the urgent inquiry into the mysterious feeling of death that led to the transmutation of Venkatraman into Bhagavan Ramana Maharshi. It is only in the fitness of things that Mother should have encountered the problem of death, though in a different way, before her true state was recognised. It was not a question of her probing a question hitherto unknown to her. "Death is forgetfulness itself," she once said. "I do not have any forgetfulness at all," she declared on another occasion. She was perfect even at birth. "I am not anything now which I was not earlier; if there is any difference, it is only in your understanding of me," she told a visitor.

Mother had completed her fourth year when Rangamma, at first seemingly recovered from her ailment, was in the seventh month of her pregnancy. But suddenly she had shooting pains in her abdomen and, within hours, she was dead. It was thought that there was some error in the treatment of the disease. Seethapathi had already left for Tenali to fetch a good doctor. He received the sad news even before he met the doctor, and immediately he rushed to Bapatla. He fell down unconscious on arrival at his house. When he recovered, he was unconsolably sorrowful. The sight of his young daughter added fuel to the fire of his sorrow, for his

heart was torn into a hundred shreds by the absolute inno-
cence of his daughter as to what had happened. She was
quiet and calm as she wiped his tears with her tender hands.

"Your mother is dead and gone forever from us," he cried
several times to his child Anasuya, not knowing how to
make her understand the situation.

"Whither has she gone, Father?" she calmly asked him.

"Yes! Whither?" he muttered to himself.

"Tell me, first of all, whence she came, Father!" she asked
him slowly, "What does dying mean?"

Failing to find a proper answer to her question, he only
repeated "She is gone!"

"But my mother is here, she has not gone anywhere!"
Anasuya pointed at the body lying on the ground.

Someone who feared that the child would be too fright-
ened if she knew the truth tried to silence her by saying,

"Oh! She is sleeping, that's all!"

"If she is sleeping, why are all these people weeping? My
mother had been sleeping every night but none had wept
before!"

The elderly intruder was dumbfounded by Anasuya's
question. Chidambara Rao took the child and Seethapathi on
to the terrace to avoid the sight of their kith and kin who were
all weeping.

"What is meant by 'dying,' Grandfather?" she asked
Chidambara Rao.

Even while he was rummaging around in his brains for a
reply, he was hit by another question:

"Whence do these people come?"

"... From out of the womb of the mother, child," he replied.

"Would there be children in the wombs of their mothers always?"

"No."

"Whence do they come there?"

"God sends them thither!"

"Then whither do they go at death?"

"To the cremation ground."

"If they are not carried to the cremation ground, would it mean that they are alive? In that case, let us keep my mother here only."

"What questions are these, child?"

"Tell me, where do they go?"

"To God."

"Why?"

"It is His will."

"If the one who was sent by God were to return to Him at His will, then why should we weep for it?"

Forgetting all the sadness of the moment in a flash, Chidambara Rao laughed and hugged Anasuya to his heart, saying, "Who has taught you all this?" Even Seethapathi looked at his child in surprise.

"You tell me, father, why should we weep?" she directed her question at him.

Perhaps she wanted to convey the idea that all the questions were meant for him and not for herself!

"But your mother is dead ..." he stammered.

"Tell me, really, who is my mother? Is she the one who has left us or is she this body? If she is the body, then she has not left us. If she is the one that has left us, then we have never seen her in fact! Then why all this agony?"

Suddenly Seethapathi and Chidambara Rao were called away to attend the last rites. Anasuya stayed behind. After a while, an elderly gentleman came to her and, taking her in his arms, showed her the body that was about to be carried to the cremation ground and asked her to bow at the body's feet, in accordance with the old custom. When the body was being actually taken away, he showed it to her saying,

"Look! She is going away."

"Why, all of them are going!" she replied, "Only she is lying and they are walking."

"But they are carrying her, and she is being carried," he said, trying to improve upon her statement.

"But we were carried together in the palanquin all the way from Mannava!" she retorted.

"Not so, silly girl! The life force that is in us is no longer there in her. That's why we say that she is gone."

"Now you say that she is gone; again, you say that she is leaving us. Tell me, is she the body or the spirit?"

"No child, I can't answer you; only your grandfather should be able to answer your questions."

A few hours later, Chidambara Rao returned from the cremation ground and was resting in the house.

"Oh! She is being burnt!" cried the girl.

"Where?" he rushed out to her in anxiety.

Anasuya was steadily gazing at the burning wick in the lamp; then she proceeded to describe every detail of the scene at the cremation ground that she had never visited before, and also the details of the rites of cremation. Chidambara Rao kept gazing at her in awe and wonder.

FOUR DAYS LATER, ANASUYA saw the pet cat of the house lying down in a strange manner under a tree.

"Grandfather, why is the cat lying like this?" she asked Chidambara Rao.

"It's about to die," he replied.

The whole body of the cat was jerking, and its nostrils were jumping.

"Why do its nostrils jump like this?" she asked him, and she applied her finger to them and lowered her head to have a closer look at the cat.

"What is this, I am seeing myself in the eye of the cat!" she cried in wonder as she looked at her own image reflected in the eyes of the cat.

"Does the cat appear in my eyes also? Just as I am seeing myself in the eye of the cat, can I not look at myself?" she asked him.

"Why not? It is but your eyes that are peeping into its eyes."

"Yes, even though it is the eyes that see, it is cognition that recognises it. That cognition is the 'I'. But why do I not see my own image directly in my own eyes?"

As she was asking questions like that, the breath of the cat suddenly stopped. Simultaneously, Anasuya found that her image in the eye of the cat grew dull.

"Oh! What has happened to the cat?" she cried.

"The cat is dead."

"Oh! Is this death? Is it the cessation of breath?"

"Life vanishes when breath stops."

"Is it the same with all?"

So asking, she applied her finger to her own nostrils and watched her breath. Gradually, her breath stopped. Chidambara Rao noticed that she had lost all awareness of the outer world. Even while he was thinking about the phenomenon deeply, she regained her normal consciousness, again applied her finger to her nostrils, and again her breath stopped. At first he was surprised, but owing to his knowledge of the uniqueness of the girl in her intelligence, mental balance, and deep insight, he wondered at the ease and control with which she could attain the state of *samadhi*.

"Whence is this Wisdom, and how long her practice?" he wondered.

All through the day, Chidambara Rao was brooding over the tragedy:

"Rangamma is no more; what a sudden change in the household! The one who was alive yesterday is no more," he was saying to himself.

The child Anasuya, who was sitting by him, said to him:

"Rangamma is but a name. Is it the name that has left us? What these people mourn for is a name and not the Mother, who is not dead; the one who died is not the mother, who is nameless. I do not perceive the mother whom they describe to have passed away. Or, did the others perceive the mother whom I could not?"

Her words paled into a muttering and finally ceased when once again she lost herself to the outer world and withdrew into the Self.

THE YEARS THAT PASSED after Anasuya's girlhood were strangely hazy. No one knows whom she met and what experiences she had bestowed on them, except that she was kept in several towns such as Guntur and Bapatla for different periods of stay with different relatives. Mostly, these moves were intended as a consolation to the young child who had lost her mother early and as a relief to Seethapathi. He could not conceive of bringing up his young ones without the assistance of his wife. But, as had already been stated, there descended on him a strange apathy and indifference regarding the ways of this growing girl. Where she went, how long she stayed away from her home, and whether she had her daily food—all these questions were strangely effaced from the minds of her guardian. I heard Mother say in a light vein that, in a way, those were the happiest and most carefree days of her life, for she was hardly restricted, much less obstructed and curiously observed, as she is today. Stray incidents involving a police constable who tried to rob her of jewellery, and who was converted into one of her most ardent devotees by a miraculous experience, came to be known by me. Another incident in which she appeared as Iswaramma (the medieval woman saint of Andhra Pradesh) to another is also recalled. Besides these incidents, not much is known about the most essential aspect of her life—the manifestation of her inner perfection.

SUPERSTITION ON TRIAL

The passage of days had not altogether effaced the sorrow of the house at the demise of Rangamma. It stabilized in the form of a passive indifference, a long-drawn stupefaction, an apathy of the various members of the family to the discharge of their duties. There was only one in the house who remained as green as ever. It was the child Anasuya.

Anasuya used to visit the temple of Lord Bhavanarayana at Bapatla. One day she visited it accompanied by her companions. While they had brought offerings to the Lord, she entered the temple empty handed. Surely, no one takes a presentation to one's own house!

"What have you brought as your offering to God? Is it the dust of your feet?" her companions asked her in a vein of ridicule and admonition. Anasuya quickly looked at her own feet and at the feet of her companions. They were all covered with the dust on which they had walked together. "The feet of those who bring an offering are as much covered with dust as of those that brought nothing!" she replied. Though the other girls hardly perceived the logic of her words, they were definitely overawed by them.

Anasuya plucked a few leaves of the tulasi plant and some flowers that were grown in the temple. Approaching the sanctum sanctorum, she kept them on the floor.

"Don't keep them on the floor; they can't be accepted for the worship of God," the priest admonished her.

"Is it the folly of those plants that they have grown on the earth?" she retorted unperturbed.

Besides the logic of what she said, even the very manner of her utterance had a ring about it that silenced him. When her companions had their coconuts broken into four halves before the idol, Anasuya perceived in the act the symbol of the One becoming two and then the many. The mystery of the unity in diversity of creation was what she had perceived in it. Giving her a bit of the coconut to eat, her companions left the temple, but Anasuya sat there. She was watching the elderly devotees come in large numbers to break coconuts. She asked a few of them to tell her why a coconut was to be broken, but only got a snub for her impudence as a reply. She sat in the temple until, in the evening, a learned pundit by name Sthanacharya arrived to expound a *purana* before an audience. Anasuya greeted him with all respect and asked him:

"Tell me, Sir, wherefrom have all these come—these flowers, the tulasi, the turmeric and the *kumkum*, the ornaments, and the garments that adorn the deity?"

Not bothering to ponder for too long about a child's prattle, he curtly replied:

"From the dust, the earth!"

"Whence the deity?" The girl would not leave him so easily.

"You mean the idol?" he asked.

"Is the idol different from God?"

"No."

"Then why speak differently about them? Whence has it come?"

"Stop these silly questions," he brushed past her.

She stayed silent at the temple till everyone had left. Even the priest did not notice her. Locking her up in the temple, he left.

Anasuya did not lose the opportunity to scrutinise the deity at close quarters, thinking to herself, "Is this stone the real God? Or do these ornaments constitute Godhead? Surely the idols look different without them. Is the earth, from which all these were derived, the real God? It supports all things; even the trees on which birds perch and build their nests are supported by the earth." So thinking, she turned her attention to the dust of her own feet and, scratching a little of it, addressed it thus:

"Mother of All, do you escape notice, while making men worship things that come from you, grow in you, and finally merge in you? Why should you, who are the source of all varieties of conscious existences, appear to be inert? My mother Rangamma had shown you to me when she left me!"

How strange are the ways of all Godmen and Godwomen! Jesus declared, "I and my Father are one," and yet prayed to the Father. Lord Krishna, being the Lord Himself, was described to have followed all religious observances in the *Mahabharata*.

Chidambara Rao was not spared the scorching attack of Anasuya's questions. He could neither answer her nor escape her. On one such occasion, he was very much vexed and so snubbed her with a rash "Keep quiet!" From then until 1947 she never spoke at home unless it was absolutely essential.

IN THE YEAR 1929, old Maridamma took Anasuya along with her to Guntur, where they stayed for a month. One day, while Anasuya was going by the road, she heard the recitation of a purana from a house. Henceforth she visited the house regularly for a month. It was the matth of a learned Swamiji by the name of Kalyanananda Bharati. The swami was surprised to note that Anasuya always came alone and sat in a corner. She did not seem to be attentive to his discourses, neither did she prostrate before him. He only recognised the unusual radiance of her face, and on the thirty-first day, he addressed her:

Swamiji: Who are you?

Anasuya: I came here to know that, because I do not know who I am.

Swamiji: What's your caste?

Anasuya: Mine is the caste of *shukla* and *shonita*.

Thus, in the course of the conversation, when the swami offered to initiate her with a *mantra*, she asked him what a mantra was.
"We charge certain syllables with divine energy and communicate the same to you in secrecy," he replied.
"If that capacity for charging the syllables is yours, you may impart the same power to a blade of grass as well!" she retorted.
The learned swami was dumbfounded! When Anasuya visited the abode of the swami the next day, someone who was irritated by her replies slapped her. The swami heard the sound and asked her, "What is that clapping sound?"

Anasuya: It is the noise of two objects coming together.

Swamiji: What do you mean?

Anasuya slapped her own cheek to demonstrate it.

Swamiji: Was that the noise of your slapping yourself, or that of another slapping you?

Anasuya: What you have heard without seeing is the

noise of someone slapping me; that which has heard while seeing, has slapped Itself.

Swamiji: Why are you late today? Why did you not come by noon?

Anasuya: The *taruna* hadn't arrived then; now it has come, and so I have come.

Swamiji: What is meant by *taruna?*

Anasuya: It is what you cannot avoid even if you wish to; it is what you cannot do even if you wish to accomplish.

In the course of the conversation, Anasuya addressed the swami as "child." When he asked her for the reason, to his utter surprise, she replied:
"That is my *vidhi*; vidhi is *vidhana*; vidhi is the Creator; His vidhana is Creation."
The swami asked Anasuya whether she was attending a school.
"I am not attending a school. I have only come to this school. This seems to be a school without a teacher!"
Obviously, this reply was a direct hit at the egoism of the swami, he being proud of learning when in fact he could not answer even one of her questions satisfactorily. Finally, when it was time for her to leave, he asked her:
"Which fruit do you like most?"
She replied:

"That ripe fruit which is not diminished by eating; that which can be enjoyed eternally—the ripe fruit of the head!" (i.e., the fruit of wisdom).

Her ready response was an eye-opener to him. He had a glimpse of what she was. He hugged her and asked:

"Who are you, Mother? Certainly you must stay with me!"

"I can't stay; you keep me with you, child," she replied in the true way of the Universal Mother.

"Won't you tell me what a mantra is?"

By thus asking her, he at last admitted his own state of incomplete knowledge.

"Then what will you be while learning?" she asked.

"Whatever you make of me!" the swami answered.

Now it was her turn to put a question to him. "Who am I, in your opinion?"

"You are Bala Rajarajeswari."

Her purpose was fulfilled. Then she answered his question about mantra: "Mantra means the Mind. The sacred syllable *(bija)* is vibration *(sabda)*. The various grades of sound are the (sacred) syllables *(akshara)*."

The swami's opinion about her was confirmed. He did not want to lose the opportunity to be accepted by her as a disciple. But, fearing that she would evade him if he asked her directly, he contrived carefully to make her act in accordance with the traditional ritual of initiation—that is, giving him, as a symbol of initiation, something to eat or drink after partaking of it herself. So, he offered her some *payasam* (porridge), and while she was drinking it, he asked her to give him a share of it. But she refused him! Instead, she enlightened him more about herself, which constituted a truer form of initiation. When he asked her about her parents, she told him that her mother's name was *adhara* and that her father was *avakasa*. When the swami wondered how an abstract, formless concept such as adhara (literally meaning the prop or basis) could be the name of an individual, she explained:

"Is not adhara a name? Is there no form to it? Take your swing, for example. The plank is supported by the chain, the chain by the beam, and the beam by the earth. There are several adhara. Everything is based upon adhara and hence all is familiar to It."

"Tell me of your real identity!" the swami cried.

"Reality itself is my state," she coolly replied.

"How do your people view you?" he asked.

"They view me as I appear to them. Mind is the measuring rod; they measure me only according to the range of their mind."

With an abrupt salutation, she took leave of him and walked out as swiftly and silently as does a vision or a revelation!

THE BRIDAL OF EARTH AND HEAVEN

It must be remembered that hours after the birth of Mother, the ladies in the family said that she should be given in marriage to Nageswara Rao. Mother, who was conscious of everything that took place about her even from the moment of her birth—in fact, even before her birth—remembered it. Marriage, according to Mother, constitutes the rejoining of the individual with the Absolute, of the soul with the Lord, and hence has an inviolable sanctity about it both in word and spirit. Hence it was that there was determination on the part of Mother also that the particular match must be settled in spite of Seethapathi's indecision in the early stages.

The marriage took place at Bapatla on 5th May 1936, precisely at the moment of sunrise (5:15 a.m.). In every detail of the ritual that the couple were asked to perform during the marriage ceremony, the innate significance must have revealed itself before those who beheld the spectacle—at least to a few of them. Mother's statements about marriage in general, the way she takes an active part in the marriages celebrated in her presence—all these are enough to afford us glimpses into her sentiments at the moment.

For instance, when the curtain was held between her and Nageswara Rao during the celebration, Mother thought of the song of the classical composer Thyagaraja in which he implored the Lord to remove the veil that separated him from Him. Similarly, during the ceremonial, the couple was made to sit side by side and a yoke was held above them. Through the small passage in it, cow's ghee was made to run down the yoke. Mother felt that the small passage symbolised the *sushumna nadi;* that the purport of the ritual was that the couple should go through the "straight gate" of life together without swerving from the passage even a little, carrying the yoke of responsibility together; that the couple symbolised the *ida* and *pingala nadis,* the right and the left, which neither is superior nor inferior to the other.

These incidents lend us an insight into Mother's philosophy of marriage, of which she is the living example to mankind.

The spiritual ministration of Mother seems to have some connection with her marriage in a way not known to us. For, before she came to be known to the world as Mother, she was given in marriage to Nageswara Rao at the age of fourteen, and Nageswara Rao, who is today addressed affectionately as "father" by all the visitors to Jillellamudi, did permit his wife to be worshipped by people as the Universal Mother. This speaks of condescension to a sublime degree. The marriage has therefore several degrees of importance. When one of the few people who recognised her innate perfection asked her why she needs to get married, she told him that it was only to show that marriage need not be feared as an obstacle to one's spiritual progress. When one had truly realised that which ought to be realised, all

ashramas—*brahmacharya, grihastha, vanaprastha,* and *sanyasa*—
are equally important. It is also to set an example of an ideal
housewife by practice that she had married—the ideal being
to be able to look upon one's life-partner as the embodiment
of the Lord (i.e., the Giver of All) and thereby realise the ultimate reality without having to suppress any of the material
aspects of personal life.

The ideal of Motherhood is no less presented by her (i.e.,
what it is to be a real Mother). By seeing the ultimate Divinity in all and seeing all as her own offspring, she sparks
the innate divinity of every soul by calling it her child.

"Who *is* the God that you worship?" someone had asked
her.

"You, my children, are the objects of my worship," she
replied.

"We are immersed in ignorance, Mother! Please save us,"
someone appealed to her in the traditional jargon.

"I do not think so, my child! In my view, you are all
perfect in wisdom," she replied.

"All of you talk of freedom from bondage and *viraga,* and
try to attain them. But look at me, I am always anxious to
have you all with me and feed you. No other desire is
there!" she once said.

What does she mean? "*Anuraga* (love) for all is real *viraga,*"
she said on some other occasion, and that explains it.

THE COUPLE DID NOT settle down together immediately after marriage. Real settlement can be taken to have materialised around 1940 when they came to live in Jillellamudi. This short period that separates the year of marriage from the year of settlement was apparently of no great significance. In fact, all the most significant periods of Mother's life remained preserved in the unwritten pages of Time, and it is only an act of grace that can unravel its mysteries. All that I could know from a visitor to Mother and some of her kith and kin—obviously the least fertile source of all valuable information—was that Mother was suspected as being mentally retarded by some, as being ill by others, as being possessed by a devil by yet others. Treatments were meted out especially by the priests of the last category, which often bordered on cruelty, and those ended only in due exposure of the hollow superstition of these curates. She was admitted in the Bayer Hospital at Chirala where she stayed considerably for a long time.

A former fellow patient one day visited Mother in 1964 in Jillellamudi. Not expecting Mother to remember her after such a long time, she asked if Mother did. Then Mother mentioned her name and the location of her bed in relation to Mother's own bed. The visitor was surprised at the precision of Mother's memory, and she went on adding her own reminiscences—how Mother was rarely in her bed but went about looking after the needs of all the other patients. She added that Mother was so much admired and loved by all the doctors and nurses that theirs was no longer the relationship of doctors, nurses, and a patient. Mother became perfect in the accomplishments of a nurse merely by observation. She also played games like tennis with the hospital staff. We were also told by the visitor—for which we should greatly be indebted to her—that a few of the European doctors looked upon Mother with the reverence and awe that is due to Christ or Mary. However, what hint the visitor had from Mother to that effect, we do not know. The visitor's account remained very inadequate and sketchy, and all efforts to extract more from her ended in evasions. She only added that Mother's form was most beautiful during that period—sublimely beautiful at that; that she never seemed to have suffered either from ailment or exhaustion however heavy her self-imposed tasks might be in the service of the patients in the hospital.

The last fragment of information that could be bagged from the visitor was that several of the patients in the hospital, and even a few of the nurses, had mystic visions and other miraculous experiences that sealed their lips, that many of them prostrated to Mother off and on in privacy, and shed tears before they took leave of her. With this inadequate picture of this period of Mother's life, we have to rest contented and turn to her arrival at Jillellamudi.

LIFE IN JILLELLAMUDI

Separated by a distance of seven miles from the nearest town of Bapatla, and by a distance of another mile and a half from the main road, even today Jillellamudi is a remote village and, but for buses, access to the village is very difficult. The journey must have presented still greater difficulties to the visitors a quarter of a century ago, when there were no regular buses and when the roads were infested by robbers. Moreover, the two culverts across the path to Jillellamudi were not constructed until recently. Those who visited the village in rains had to wade through very deep and fast running streamlets.

The village was faction ridden and was divided in the early days of Mother's arrival. The hostility of most of the villagers towards Nageswara Rao and his family was because he did not inherit the post of a Karanam but was appointed. The hostility of the inhabitants always meant harm to the members of this family. It was under such circumstances that Mother had to live there, spending days in loneliness when Nageswara Rao was away from the village on work. She was looking after the needs of the family, doing all the domestic work herself: fetching water from the freshwater tank at the end of the village, making dung cakes for fuel, making ropes out of fibre, tending and milking the cattle, receiving visitors to the family and to the village, etc. Those who had seen and recognised her for what she was in those early days recount how tender Mother looked. They were surprised to see such a tender lady attending to stupendous tasks all by herself, never complaining or feeling them to be a burden. Owing to the meagre resources of the family, she was very simple in her dress. She wore very ordinary sarees and was found to relax on the rugged floor or on a very short and narrow wooden box. Very fair in complexion, tender in build, her hair very dark and reaching to her knees, she is said to have resembled Sita Devi (the Consort of Lord Rama) living in Parnasala. Never looking tired however hard her tasks were, she was very affectionate and kind towards all.

The profundity of her wisdom, the inner perfection, was well concealed behind the infinite modesty, dutifulness, and simplicity of a village housewife. Very few could even suspect her of being what she is; for she never broached any discussion or talk concerning the Truth with anyone. But if anyone tried to pretend to be a master of wisdom, he was shown his proper place promptly and with a perfect economy of words.

The early visitors were surprised to find the large number of dogs and cats that were moving about the house in perfect harmony and friendship. There were as many as fifteen cats. Two of them were specially conspicuous by their extraordinary behaviour. One of them used to address Mother as "Amma" (mother) in a very clear voice. Another used to attend to its bodily needs only once in a fortnight, resting on all the other days on a rafter just above the place where Mother rested. Towards the end of its life, it went on repeating the *pranava* mantra *OM* loudly and incessantly for three days before it breathed its last. Similarly, one of the dogs used to suckle even the kitten along with its own pups. A few of the dogs used to lead visitors from the bus stop to the village and again followed them up to the bus stop on their return. Mother used to address the animals by names. Equally surprising to the visitor was the fact that, while Mother rested on the floor after her daily chores, rats used to play on the pallu, the loose end of her sari, and the cats rested all about her.

More uncanny was the mystery of an anthill in a corner of the house in which a cobra lived. No one ever saw the cobra but they found that Mother was leaving a little coffee, boiled rice, or even peeled plantains before it. After some time, these were found to be missing; sometimes only a portion of them was gone, with clear markings of the serpent's fangs on what remained. Occasionally a beam of light emanated from one of the openings of the anthill, illuminating a portion of the house. At one time, one of the villagers joined as a servant in the house with very sinister designs in his heart toward the family. But he was transformed by what he saw. One day, in the early hours of dawn, he found Mother standing attentively in the middle of the house. Before her he saw a strange serpent, not more than a foot in length and with an extraordinary large hood.

Strange light emanating from the anthill was illuminating the whole house. The serpent was very rapidly whirling round and round in mid air before Mother. The servant Subbaiah could no longer control himself. He prostrated before her, weeping loudly and cursing himself for the sinister designs of his heart. Even today one can see Subbaiah dedicating himself to the service of the visitors.

Years later, another pious woman who visited Mother reported a similar glimpse of an extraordinary snake. Yet another spoke of two such snakes—one of them golden in its glitter and the other silvery. Whenever references were made to those serpents or questions were raised, Mother was mostly reticent. When she was pressed for an explanation, she only said that it was an experience those visitors needed.

The earliest of the servants to be employed in Mother's house was an agile young man named Mantrai. He was notorious for his criminality. Yet, soon after coming into her service, he was transformed. He was found listening to the illuminating talks of Mother with tears overflowing from his eyes. Every moment of his life, wherever he might be, he could see the form of Mother clearly before him as she was at that moment at her house. He could readily perceive any need of his service at home without being sent for by Mother. At the moment of his death, he advised Subbaiah (referred to previously) never to leave Mother's service.

The transformation of these individuals marked a change

in the attitude of the other inhabitants of the village. Besides, Mother was actively interested in the needs of the villagers. It was a very backward village, and almost all its inhabitants were very poor. They had to live by manual labour in the agricultural season. Once the season was over, their resources dwindled rapidly and they had to spend most of the days in starvation. Therefore, Mother organised something like a grain "bank." During the season of their employment (and during the harvest), every villager was to contribute a handful of rice every day to the bank, which was managed by Mother. During the lean months, anyone that was in need could draw his rations from her and replace them later when they had the means to contribute. In addition to this, she was giving food to every visitor to the village. Thus, she came to be known as the Mother to the villagers.

The village had been declared to be unfit for the location of a temple by the orthodox people several decades earlier. But Mother, in course of time, purchased a piece of land on which a temple is now under construction. In this connection we must remember the resolve that Mother had made as a child, i.e., to erect a temple in a place where there is none. The number of visitors increased steadily, and people were pouring into the village from all neighbouring towns. As many as a dozen officials used to visit the village every weekend from Chirala. Similar batches of visitors came to her regularly from neighbouring villages such as Poondla and

Kommur. These early batches had greater opportunities to bask in the warm sunlight of Mother's physical presence than present-day visitors, for they were fewer in number. Besides, Mother used to cook for them and serve food to them personally. Today they recount the unique flavours and tastes of the variety of dishes she made with all kinds of leaves—even of the cotton plant, grasses, and of the neem tree! They used to arrive at Jillellamudi by Saturday afternoon and spend all the time in the presence of Mother until the evening of Sunday. They posed several questions, and argued and discussed with her for the sheer joy of being thrilled by her simple, profound, and effortless replies. Their lives are rich storehouses of divine experiences, which they would never reveal to anyone in all their entirety. Some of them started by advising her to get initiated by their spiritual guides; others tried to be her doctors; yet others tried to enlighten her by their discourses. They only ended up with tears flowing from their eyes and their hands joined together in salutation.

As the number of visitors steadily increased, the common dining hall "Annapurna" came to be founded on the 15th of August 1958 in the service of the visitors. Thus, another of Mother's early resolutions materialised. It must be mentioned that the food that one is served here is certainly not luxurious. It is not possible to serve a great variety of dishes in a village where nothing is available and where everything has to be fetched across a distance of nine miles. It is essentially a means of sustaining a seeker after enlightenment during his stay, and certainly not intended to sustain and multiply the demands of his palate.

Thus, at present, a visitor to Jillellamudi finds that all his requirements are met—food and shelter are provided for him during his stay there, and certainly Mother's love is the one luxury that he is sure to enjoy—for, everyone, whatever his caste or creed or social status, has free access to Mother. He can discuss and argue with Mother on anything, if he so pleases. No reservations or inhibitions need be there to enjoy the bliss of Mother's love.

Many of the visitors slowly came to settle at Jillellamudi, and today they number nearly one hundred. They spend their time in the presence of Mother and in the service of new visitors. They welcome everyone into their brotherhood.

No one is a "visitor" or a guest there. Everyone is a member of the brotherhood. No one enjoys special privileges except the sick and the ailing. No one is high and no one is low there. No one is the servant and no one the master. Everyone serves himself, his brothers, and his sisters. Work and service are a matter of pride there and not demeaning. The want of this spirit of brotherhood, equality, and service subjects no one to any criticism or insult save that of his own conscience. It is the house of all. Even the cats, dogs, and the cattle of that place are heirs to this divine brotherhood, and it is our fault if we fail to enjoy it.

CHAPTER II

The House of All—A Symbol
of Synthesis

MASTERS OF PERFECT ATTAINMENT say that the different paths to
perfection such as jnana, bhakti, and karma yoga have a
fundamental unity. When one pursues one of the three,
the other two follow of their *own* accord, said Bhagavan
Ramana Maharshi. The unique greatness of the *Bhagavad
Gita* seems to be this synthesis of these paths. For, Lord
Krishna not only expounded their unity but symbolised it
in Himself. He is called the *Yogiswara, Jagadguru,* and the
Jagannatha, i.e., he is at once the ideal and the goal of the
three paths of jnana, bhakti, and karma yoga. We find this
unity of all paths propounded by Mother and exemplified
in herself. There can be no greater illustration of this fact
than the House of All that grew around her at Jillellamudi.
That this House of All was not a chance establishment but
was premeditated by Mother is evident from the resolu-
tion that she had arrived at as a girl—to establish a free
lodging and boarding house, besides a Sanskrit school and
a temple.

What one finds to be most conspicuous besides Mother herself at Jillellamudi is the House of All. It does not in the slightest degree resemble a choultry or a restaurant. It is a universal family in which the visitor will not be treated as a stranger but as a member of the brotherhood. From the elderly inmates of this Universal family to the tiniest tot, everyone is addressed and treated as a brother or sister by everyone else.

"Everyone has his family. But all those families together constitute the universal family," Mother once remarked.

No guilty thoughts find their shelter behind any hypocritical shyness between the brothers and sisters. The universal family is a different world of its own kind, utterly unlike the world in which one generally finds himself imprisoned at birth. The new visitors are often struck by the informality, cordiality, and the familiarity with which he is received into their brotherhood by both the brothers and sisters. Even if the cobwebs of one's sinful world stick to one like burrs, soon one is freed from them, or else one will find himself so utterly unfit for the place that he dare not set his foot again in it till repentance has burnt out the evil.

The inmates of the House of All are drawn from various walks of life and various classes of society. We are likely to be surprised to see a simple person turning out to be a wealthy one or a great scholar, who has preferred the hard work of looking after the needs of the new visitors to the place as being more ennobling than mere enjoyment of wealth. Many of them had considered the simplicity, sanctity, and the cordiality of this place as being far more attractive than what they had "sacrificed" in the eyes of the world. There are nearly a hundred resident members in the House of All. All of them attend to some work or the other and are never idle. They are ever up and working to provide for the necessities of the visitors. They fetch hundreds of pots of water from a nearby tank for drinking. They attend to cultivation of acres of land. They do all the manual labour necessary in the construction of the buildings for lodging the visitors. They cook and serve food to them.

Waking up hours before sunrise to join the recital of the *Suprabhata* to the Holy Mother, they put in continuous hours of hard work, which astounds even a man of the strongest build. What is more, more than half of them are girls. Neither the sweltering summer nor the biting cold of winter, not even the incessant downpours of the rainy season can force them to swerve from their duty. In spite of such hard work, all that they eat is a chutney, tamarind water, and buttermilk. They do not enjoy even the minimum of comforts like warm rugs, soft beds, hot-water bath, etc. But they always live more happily than those who have them, and are never conscious of the simplicity of their lives. No one asks them or compels them to work. They derive no personal benefit out of it. They do not get any gratitude from the visitors who often mistake them for labourers. They had identified themselves too well with toil even to realise that gratitude is due to them. They enjoy no special privileges either with other inmates of the House of All or from Mother. They find no time even to sit for a few minutes with Mother everyday. But it is always the chant of Mother's name that dances on their lips; it is always the very vividly felt presence of Mother constantly by their side that opens for them the floodgates of the infinite energy that renders any strenuous task a mere matter of play. If you ask them "Where do you get such strength? How do your limbs stand the strain?" they reply, "We don't feel any; when we return, it is the Mother's body that aches for all that we do—if it is we that do that work!"

Years might have passed since their arrival at Jillellamudi. Even the prospect of a short spell of their absence from Jillellamudi is a terrible catastrophe in their view. One of the girls lost her father while she was at Jillellamudi. When the news was brought to her, she wept, not so much for her father's death but at the possibility of her being kept away at her home. Only strong assurances by her relatives that she would be sent back to Jillellamudi in a couple of days could divert her sorrow towards her father who was no more.

All that these children of Mother know is that they could not bear the separation from Mother. Her presence is the reward of all that they do, and no other desire ever makes its appearance in their minds. In their toil, we find the practical demonstration of the oneness of all the paths—bhakti, karma, and jnana—of which Mother herself is the visible manifestation. All the toil that they perform is based on the intense self-denying love of Mother's nearness. That constitutes bhakti or devotion. The toil that they do is selfless—the very perfection of karma yoga wherein it is not action that is relinquished but the fruit of action. Their absolute unwavering faith in Mother, their continuous awareness of her divinity, the absence of any longing in them for anything else—these constitute their *vairagya* and *viveka*. The Christian ideal of service is more than achieved in them. In the unceasing music of their divine labours the thraldom of all worldly attachments and desires is broken. I was one of those who looked upon them as the unwise, non-spiritual busybodies who prefer a sidetracking task as being far more engrossing than undivided spiritual quest in the form of meditation and austerities.

"Do you suppose that the mind can be separated from all sensuous desires merely by running into a forest, or by closing of the eyes?" Mother echoed my unspoken thoughts.

"What happened to the great masters in penance, such as Visvamitra, Agastya, and others? Sensual pleasures are the very matrix of creation. They are the cause of your birth; you are a product of that. Even the animals that move around you in the lonely forests are enough to taunt you with your innate emotions and desires. Certainly the almost continuous hard work that these girls do, their continuous chanting of the divine name, their faith, their selflessness, and their austerely simple lives are far more efficacious instruments of their inner purification than the mere closing of the eyes of one who has none of these aids to save him from his own passions and cravings."

I was initiated by Mother's words into a more impartial self-examination and prayed that I should deserve as much attention from Mother towards my spiritual development as those inmates of the House of All. For, theirs is the yoga of devotion and *japa;* theirs is *dhyana,* theirs is the divine fruit of *nishkama karma* and *viveka.* Even they do not know the infinitude of the treasures of Bliss to which they are heirs. It is rather a deep-seated and vague perception of that by their intuitions that perhaps binds them so inextricably to Mother and to Jillellamudi.

As with their bodies, so with their minds. Despite the incredibly hard work that they attend to throughout the day, they still have the zeal in them to devote the one or two hours of their rest to the study of Sanskrit. A Sanskrit school was founded in 1966 for that purpose. All of them passed the examination in first class. Today you can hear them conversing freely and fluently in Sanskrit among themselves.

"They are not merely my children; they are my limbs," said Mother once.

Though the "children" of Mother are rarely conscious of the fact, Mother has a definite purpose and a method in entrusting them with so much work. Once she explained her purpose:

"Theirs is the time to come. All of my children must know all kinds of work. There should be nothing which they cannot do. Whatever be the nature and habits of the men that they might marry in future, they should be perfect in moulding their (domestic) life accordingly. If the husband happens to be a drunkard, the girl should hand him the cup with joy; they must adjust within their means. Instead of complaining of what they do not have, they should have the resourcefulness to make the best of what they have. They attain perfection through the perfect discharge of their duties. For example, the winnowing basket is the "fifth *Veda*." We are within ourselves just as the rice is within the paddy. We should get separated from the chaff of our flaws in a like manner; there are as many truths hidden within us as there are in a grain of paddy!"

Obviously, what Mother is preparing them for is the ideal life of a housewife, for an ideal marriage. "To a woman, husband is God in human form. That faith is the easiest means for Liberation. Creating the form of an invisible God in the mind, worshipping it in mountain fastnesses, falling a prey to suppressed (not conquered) desires, even a *muni* cannot accomplish what an ordinary housewife can easily accomplish, and she needs no special mantra or *sadhana* for it."

If this is so with Mother's daughters, how about her sons? Well, it's all the same. Just as a woman should worship her husband as God's manifestation, he should endeavour to see God in his wife. This does in no way prejudice the conjugal relationship between the couple. In fact, God as the bestower of all wishes and necessities is more completely symbolised therein. Only the attitude of respect, sanctity, and devotion should be there, and marriage should not be a licence for mere lust. Besides, Mother seems to imply that God alone is the *purusha* or the Lord, and that all Creation is *prakriti* or his Consort; each individual creature is His consort and finds the completeness of its perfection only by being absorbed into Him through devotion. Viewed in this perspective, marriage is different from legalised sex-indulgence in that it is pre-eminently symbolic of the divine union with the "Beloved," as the Sufis call Him. When this symbol is recognised by the couple and adhered to, both attain perfection without the need for all artificial suppressions of the natural urges. The truth and possibility of such a marriage is amply established by the case of Sri Ramakrishna Paramahamsa and Sarada Devi.

THE HOUSE OF ALL was established on the 15th of August 1958 to cater to the needs of the new visitors. The dozens of early visitors all enjoyed the hospitality of Mother and Nageswara Rao, the latter whom they affectionately address as "Father." Today, hundreds of devotees and visitors come daily, have their food in the free boarding house, and reside in the lodging rooms. Every drop of water that they drink, every morsel of food that they eat, every inch of the rooms in which they sleep had all been anointed by the piety and the devotion of those blessed children of Mother who bless the visitor by calling him as one of their brethren and welcome him into their fold.

As for the new visitors who arrive at the House of All, those who stay there sufficiently long would assist the inmates in their tasks. No one asks a visitor to do anything, but most of them, when Mother had retired into her inner apartments, find greater joy and benefit in lending the inmates a helping hand. For one thing, the place affords them a chance to render real service to their brethren, which they are prevented from doing elsewhere owing to the prudish habits and ways of our world. Without reservation, they can let their minds and bodies bow in humility and take delight in their inner self being noble. This joining with the band of workers further secures the mind of the visitors from idle wandering and prevents them from being too curious about the ways of others. In fact, the charm of the brotherhood that is found in that service is such that many a visitor desires to stay in Jillellamudi for that purpose.

During the first few visits, the visitor might retain the taint of prudishness of the outer world, but he soon realises that to be the greatest obstacle in the way of realising himself, in the way of communicating with the divine springs of service that lie in him. The visitor soon realizes that, when he attends to work, the body, which with all its habits and fleshly evils, becomes the greatest distraction of the mind when left to itself, is kept too busily occupied to be able to disturb the mind from its constant dwelling on Mother. The mind and body at once do the service of Mother. At the end of a few days' work, he realises how the hard shell of his egoism and vanity had been completely dissolved. The inner spirit feels the fresh beauty of and the natural wonder at life and creation, which the newly hatched chick would feel. The mind is gently and constantly caressed by the breezes of inner purity and simplicity. Christ said that one must become innocent and pure as a child before one can enter the kingdom of heaven. This is the change that is wrought in us by work. We realise why traditional religion laid stress on devoted and selfless service to God, to humanity, and to the spiritual Guide.

CHAPTER III

The Miracle That Is Mother

MOTHER DID NOT RENOUNCE the world and certainly had not shunned it. "Real viraga" she described as "love for all" (*anuraga*). She does not wear the ochre robes but she dons only sarees. Her hair is not matted. It is well combed and dressed, and often flowers are worn by her. In short, she is a perfect housewife wearing all the usual ornaments. For, of what use are the ochre robes and the matted hair to one who is herself the embodiment of Existence–Knowledge–Bliss, the One to realize whom ascetics and yogis undertake these paths? It must be remembered that the dress of a sanyasi is not a symbol of one's inner dispassion but is only a means to that. As Mother puts it, sanyasa is not something that can be adopted; it is a state of being. Once that is attained, no external observances are necessary. To quote Mother again, "One can live in *samsara*; but samsara should not be allowed to dwell in us." From her birth to the present day, she never asked for anything—even in her childhood. She never complained or tried to escape any suffering, however severe. Can there be a greater sanyasi? When anyone exclaimed to her "How great is your forbearance!" she replied:

"The question of forbearance arises if at all there is any suffering!"

Mother was once asked whether she has any disciples. She replied:

"I have no *sishyas* (disciples); all are my *sisus* (children) only."

When once someone asked Bhagavan Ramana Maharshi whether he had any disciples, one of his disciples answered on his behalf: "The Maharshi does not regard any as being outside himself and therefore none can be disciple to him."

Mother explained what motherhood is when she said, "Motherhood does not stand for mere womanhood; Mother is the Infinite, the Eternal Basis of all existence; that which is All, and cannot be understood."

"Real motherhood does not merely consist of the realisation of motherhood in oneself. Motherhood must be established in everything."

Mother does not and never did perform any spiritual practices. For, she is the direct manifestation of that Supreme state that is said to be attained through those practices. When someone asked her whether we can attain perfection through her, she replied:

"What is there to be attained through me? I am the Mother. What is there to be attained through Mother? Seeing Mother *is* attaining!"

Does she speak freely with the visitors? Does she teach anything? Yes! She does the former but not the latter. One can talk with her as freely as one does with one's own mother.

She talks more affectionately than our own mothers. A poet rightly described her as the Mother that overshadows all mothers by her Motherhood. Even animals reveal unusual awareness of her Motherliness in her presence. Any question might be put to her, and no bold discussion with her would ever be scorned or treated as impertinent.

Mother does not give any lectures or preachings:

"Tell us something, Mother," requested a visitor, "so that we might attain perfection by practising it."

"What is the use of merely talking?" she replied, "What is needed should be done."

She implies that all necessary changes in us would be wrought by her, and nothing is left to our effort. When a similar request was made to Ramana Maharshi, he said, "Why should you burden yourselves with more knowledge? Is it so as to suffer more?" and added, "That Supreme state which is obtained here and now as a result of association with a sage cannot be gained with the aid of a guru or through knowledge of the scriptures, or by spiritual merit or by any other means .... To what purpose are various methods of self-discipline?" If that is so with a sage, it must be much more so with Mother who assured us, "Seeing Mother is attaining."

HOW DOES MOTHER LOOK? That shall be the last question to be taken up. For, her physical form is as wonderful as herself. Certainly, anyone who observes her closely would be knowing that she is not her body. Perhaps this is what she hinted at when she told someone:

"Mother does not mean the Mother that is sitting on a cot in Jillellamudi only. Mother is That which has no beginning and no end, and That which is the Beginning and the End."

Of a short stature, Mother can be said to be of the stature of a medium-sized deity in the temple. Even her features, her chin, the shape of the head, and the general cut of the body is like that of the goddess that is generally installed in the temples with only one difference; that is, she has a prominent stomach. Passing her hand about it, she often says laughingly that she is pregnant always and that she is always the new mother; she goes on to trace and count innumerable babies inside her belly by a movement of her hand about it. It recalls to mind the description of the Universal Mother as one who is pregnant with the whole universe in her womb.

Her complexion is unusually radiant, though not so fair as it once was. But the most mysterious feature of it is that her complexion changes constantly, often to match any colour of the clothes that her devotees offer her. So often and so completely does her general appearance change that, to verify whether these changes are but the projections of personal imagination, one devotee took a dozen photos of Mother at a time. Strangely enough, the photos revealed such differences in her appearance that, in some, she looked like a teenager, and in some she looked like an old woman. No two photos resembled each other greatly. This change is not what is "made" in herself by herself in the way of the demonstration of a miracle, but it goes on all the time. Only the visitors do not perceive it closely. The perceiver in them is lost at the sight of Mother, and often they are too much beside themselves to do so. She seems to incarnate the very phenomenon of change, which Creation is, in herself.

Her face is most striking by its brilliance, and it radiates peace and calm as it were. There is a distant familiarity about it to everyone; yet there is something new about her face so that either consciously or unconsciously the visitor's gaze goes on searching out for the cause. It is very common to see most visitors fix their gaze on her for a very long time and that without the least movement of their eyelids! This happens not only to grown-ups but even to very young children. The remarkably big round dot of kumkum is another aspect that strikes the visitor. Well poised between the eyebrows instead of being a mere beauty spot in the centre of the forehead, the very sight of it suggests to the mind the idea of Motherhood.

Her round and elegantly shaped arms and fingers impart a novel unearthly beauty to the brightly coloured bangles and the rings that she wears. The hands have, in their touch, a new force so that the very pass of her hand on one's head would fill one's heart with the abundance of maternal affection and love that swallows up all other vexations and sorrows of life. Her feet too are unusually beautiful in their shape and delicate in the texture of the skin. Once an ardent devotee of Lord Rama by the name of Rangamma Babu came to see Mother.

"Did you notice her feet? You will not find such feet any-where else! Is it so easy to come across such holy feet?" he exclaimed to everyone by his side and added that noth-ing more is needed to testify to her divinity. Here the scepti-cal reader must remember that the ancient mystic lore is full of the detailed descriptions of the various signs to be found only on the body of a divine manifestation, such as the thirty-two marks on the body of the Buddha, as described in the ancient Buddhist texts.

The delicateness of her body is one of the most unusual features. It is as delicate as that of a newborn baby. Even if a devotee lightly presses her feet in bowing before them, they remain bloodshot for a long time after. Yet, when she chooses, she displays such vigour and resistance that even the most athletic fail to meet her challenge in endurance and efficiency in working. How she combines in herself the extremes of delicacy and strength is a marvel. For, she is often seen to enter the kitchen room and thrust her hand deep into boiling *sambar* to take out the pieces of vegetables from its depths. Even the most experienced cook uses large-handled utensils for this job. Once, when some devotees wanted to bathe her in milk as an *abhisheka*, the villagers also rushed to seize the opportunity for joining in the festivity, and in their fear that such an occasion might not be offering itself again, some brought milk that had not cooled from boiling in pots, pouring the steaming milk on her head. She neither moved nor was affected at all. Even afterwards, she never displayed any signs of burn or pain.

Similarly, some devotees once wanted to perform worship with various kinds of leaves, perhaps to visualize in her a goddess of vegetation and nature. These leaves contained some varieties that cause deadly itching on account of their hairs and sap. The hands of those that offered them were swollen with itching, but she was not affected at all. There is also a case of big stones being thrown by a deranged devotee at her from the distance of a few yards as he felt like doing her puja with stones! She never denied him the pleasure.

The absolute fluidity of her form and excellence is nowhere better illustrated than by the fact that whatever be her mood at a particular moment, she seems to be the very manifestation of that mood itself. If she was angry, her very look is sufficient to pin down a man to the few inches of ground on which he stands. For hours he would be finding it difficult to stir unless she unlocks his nerves on resuming a more benign aspect. At such moments one would doubt whether she was not the manifestation of the terrible or the angry aspect of God and wonder whether she would ever smile. Again, when she is gay and playful, one would find in her a childlike joy and mischief, and she seems to be the very manifestation of mirth; she would joke with and mimic those with whom she speaks. None would, at such a moment, believe that she can ever be terrible in her aspect. In her mimicry, she is just the person whom she mimics; it looks as though she were proving to us that all forms are hers, and from her own gestures all forms have come to be!

One more surprising aspect of Mother's physical form is that she sometimes appears to be very tall and sometimes very short, not just to individuals but to several people at a time! Whether she really is taller at those moments, I never had the presence of mind needed to verify.

The difference in her physical proportion at various times in a day are clearly illustrated. One day, someone offered her a sari and a blouse that he already had a tailor stitch. It was found to be too small for her. "I did not know your measurement, Mother!" the visitor apologised with a disappointed heart. "No one knows my measure. I am the measure of all," she said, playing on that word to convey a deep mystical meaning. She was implying that proportion and harmony, and the resulting forms, all proceed from the One that manifested itself as all. But the visitor felt sad that his offering proved not to fit Mother. In a short while, Mother finished her bath and came out with the sari and blouse that he had brought. He did not notice the blouse as he already thought it to be useless. But she told him that it fit perfectly on her! And to his surprise he found indeed that it no longer was too tight but just suited her. Similarly, on several occasions, I have seen that the bangles someone had offered proved too small for her hands at one moment but slipped over easily to their proper place a few moments later.

Finally, it must be admitted that Mother's form is really wonderful, and that the real wonder does not consist in any of these aforesaid aspects, which in themselves are miraculous enough, but lies behind them. Her form speaks the language of the spirit. It is like the shape of a flame, having a form, yet capable of assuming several forms. She shines, sitting on her cot inside a simple thatched hut in an insignificant village in South India, as the very meaning of Creation. She seems to be the visible manifestation of "The word was with God and the word was God." She is at once the hub and the wheel of Time. She seems to personify the unity underlying the diversity that is Creation.

THE BAPTISM OF TEARS

Why is it that we are drawn irresistibly into the presence of Mother again and again when once we have visited her? Before we had seen her, our life was a quest for something that we did not know; after the first visit to Jillellamudi, it becomes a quest for the inner solace that we had experienced in her presence. It is a quest for something we finally know but don't find anywhere else. In her company, we experience that life has been unburdened; we feel that our personality, for the first time, is expanding like vast space, made pure as the sky, blissful as the fresh flowers of the spring season. We feel that our mind is stilled as the still flame and brightened as the morning sun. In her presence, we feel the Purity and the Bliss that we originally are, and clearly cognise the difference between what we were before and after visiting Mother. It is for this that we visit her again and again! "The Guru is quiet and peace prevails in all"— we are reminded of these words of Ramana Maharshi. And of these: "The cosmic mind manifesting in some rare sage is able to effect the linkage of the individual mind with the inner Self."

On closer observation of one's experience in the presence of Mother, one finds that the innumerable problems that vex the mind in our day-to-day life, and the myriad purposeless musings and observations in which the mind loses itself every day, are all arrested. The mind is calmed just as a busy city calms down at the onset of the night. Quiet peace prevails; after-thoughts still wander on the vistas of the mind, yet they are only a few, like solitary night-walkers, and are mostly confined to Mother, her greatness, and the observation of the activities at the Ashram. Quite imperceptibly, the mind is drawn closer and closer to the state of one-pointedness for which we strive in vain by ourselves. The whole period of our stay becomes, as it were, a steady flow of purity, calm, and bliss. In short, *sadhana* automatically goes on in us without our effort and perhaps without our noticing! Her miraculous form, her incomparable words, her profound silence, her joy—these enchant the visitor's mind and keep him spellbound to one object of thought— the miracle that is Mother.

One extraordinary experience that is most commonly shared by the majority of the visitors is the sudden gushing of a strange, indescribable emotion that brings about a flow of tears from one's eyes, the quivering of the lips and the chin. Sometimes a visitor is found loudly weeping either while prostrating before her feet or while leaning in her lap. Even the one who experiences this will not be able to explain or express the reason for it but undergoes the experience—even repeatedly sometimes! Once I made bold to ask Mother why most of the people who come to her weep in her presence. On several occasions she evaded an answer; at others, she simply hinted at it by passing an unrelated remark that real goodness of the other brings tears to one's eyes and makes one weep. But when once I pressed her for a proper reason, she said that the reason for their weeping is the same as the one for a child's cry at its birth.

"Does it mean that your darshan marks a rebirth of the inner being?" someone asked.

"Yes," she said. "In fact that is not sorrow at all. Ordinary sorrow has a reason for it, but this has none. You call it weeping only for want of a better word to describe it. It is not real weeping!"

It must be remarked here that one's age, status, or the

inner ability to suppress one's feelings are of no avail when once Mother tickles that mysterious experience in us, throwing open the floodgates of the heart. The moments following that strange experience come nearest to one's intellectual conception of the word *samadhi*. When I later pondered over it, I was reminded of the *Bhakti Sutras*, which describe the flow of tears, choking of the voice, and the quivering of the body as being the external signs of intense bhakti.

This flow of tears is experienced sometimes at the first sight of Mother, sometimes during one's prolonged stay, and sometimes while taking leave of her. That she has a direct control and command of the fountainhead of the feelings in our hearts, I had ample experience and proof. I had it when I boasted that I am the only one who could restrain it and be unaffected by such a feeling. I had seen that the glance Mother casts on us sometimes sparks off the explosive emotion. On one occasion, puja was going on, and Mother was sitting on the platform raised for the purpose. I was also there. When Mother glanced at me once, I suddenly became sad, and I was surprised at what I thought was a coincidence. She purposefully kept her eyes away from me. I did not know why. When I was thinking so, she glanced at me a second time, and then, tears suddenly rimmed my eyelids! My voice choked, and my brain became tense owing to my efforts to restrain and suppress the tears. Then I knew why she did not look at me for long. I was so trapped in an inner crux between the intense emotion and the effort to suppress, that I inwardly prayed to Mother to let out the feeling rather than leave me in the hellish trap. Then she turned her gaze in my direction and fixed it on me. Tears rolled freely from my eyes. I was immensely relieved of my inner tension, and I knew that our feelings were entirely at her command.

On several occasions I had seen her visitors who, feeling too shy to allow their tears to flow freely, became subject to unbearable inner tension. Then Mother calls them near and gently touches their head. There comes an outburst of their feeling and they cry, burying their heads in her lap or bowing at her feet. Some of them continue in the same mood for quite a long time, and there are others who, during the several days of their stay, experience a profuse flow of tears whenever they allow their gaze to rest on her form for a few moments at a stretch. It is really a matter of her grace that laymen like us, who hardly succeed in pursuing sadhana with any consistency, are suddenly wafted into such heights of spiritual exaltation that the outward signs of intense bhakti (see Narada's *Bhakti Sutras*) manifest in us just by the sight of her form, or her touch, or even by a word addressed to us by Mother. It is the veritable baptism of tears!

WHAT IS THE BASIS of such an experience? The following words of Bhagavan Ramana Maharshi seem to contain the clue to it:

"Association with the wise will make the mind sink into the Heart. Such association is both mental and physical."

"The extremely visible being (of the guru) pushes the mind inward. He is in the heart of the seeker and so he draws the latter's inward-bent mind into the heart."

The gist of this is conveyed by what Mother said when she was asked by someone whether perfection can be attained through her (Mother).

"What is there to be attained through me? I am the Mother. Seeing Mother *is* attaining!"

Finally, we shall conclude by noting this conversation of a devotee with Ramana Maharshi:

Disciple: Horripilation, sobbing voice, joyful tears, etc., are mentioned in *Atma Vidya Vilaasa* and other works. Are these found in samadhi, or before or after?

Maharshi: All these are the symptoms of exceedingly subtle modes of mind (vrittis) ... Samadhi is perfect peace where these cannot find place. After emerging from samadhi, the remembrance of the state gives rise to these symptoms. In bhakti marga, these are the precursors to samadhi.

Mother, when questioned about it, said that people weep before her for the same reason for which they weep when they were born, thereby signifying that visiting her constitutes a spiritual rebirth. Let us see what Bhagavan Ramana Maharshi said to amplify the same truth:

"That fact of the ego rising from the Self and forgetting
it is birth ... The present desire to regain one's mother
is in reality the desire to regain the Self, which is the
same as realising oneself, or the death of the ego; this
is surrender unto the Mother ..."

THE SUBTLE ALCHEMY

The first visit to Jillellamudi bestows the silent initiation of
Mother. The shorter or longer stay in her presence bestows
inner peace culminating in the baptism of tears. These two
experiences mark a turning point in one's life, the beginning
of a subtle inner alchemy that goes on within one's heart,
independent of Mother's physical proximity. For they establish an unbreakable inner link with the universal Self of
which Mother's physical form is a visible manifestation.
Even afterwards, one vaguely feels her presence, often as a
mere thought in his mind that is ever present as the back-
ground of all other thoughts even while he is physically
separated from her by a great distance. It is not a passive
presence, though. It is subtle and subtly powerful. Its activity, like the movement of a swiftly rotating top, is hidden
beneath the appearance of stability. The presence, like the
rotating top, attracts to itself all thoughts, feelings, and
musings, and gives the whole of one's deeper personality a
new orientation and a new shape.

When one comes back to Jillellamudi after his first visit and his first stay, vivid memories of Mother's form, words, and gestures, and a memory of the bliss that he experienced in her presence stick to his mind and do not fall off. The seed strikes root and grows, with new "routes" of experience opening down into one's heart. Only when I knew this could I comprehend what Sri Sai Baba of Shirdi meant when he said:

"My tomb will speak and move with those who make me their sole refuge" and "Even after my *mahasamadhi*, I shall be with you, the moment you think of me, at any place."

Bhagavan Ramana Maharshi said:

"Association with the wise will make the mind sink into the Heart. Such association is both mental and physical. The extremely visible being (of the guru) pushes the mind inward. He is in the heart of the seeker and so he draws the latter's inward-bent mind into the heart."

As time passes, the mental association grows and finally swallows up all other worldly associations. The petty jealousies and vexations of personal and official life are rendered lifeless. One is in the least contact possible with the world mentally and lives, as it were, in her presence. How significant this change is can be understood from what Mother said to someone who sadly complained that the pressure of circumstances prevented him from visiting her frequently:

"It is enough if the mind is here. It matters little where the body is."

On another occasion she said: "*Dhyasa* is *dhyana*" (active remembrance is dhyana), and one's attention fixed on Mother constitutes dhyana. It is to this involuntary progress of sadhana without one's individual effort that Mother refers when she says:

"*Sadhana* is the accomplishment of what yields (of it-self) to accomplishment (*sadhya*)."

She defined *jijnasa* (the desire to know) as "yearning" or "pining." The intense longing to see and be with Mother, which is heightened by one's incapacity to go there, consti-tutes this pining or yearning. This pining is but a manifesta-tion of the intense longing for the perfect peace and bliss that one had enjoyed in her presence.

Bliss and peace are said to characterise Liberation or *moksha*. Mother said that intense desire for Liberation is it-self Liberation. She meant that unless one is liberated from the desire for the worldly objects of enjoyment, one does not experience real desire for Liberation, and once this real desire for Liberation is experienced, one can be sure of at-taining it. Even in the case of the devotee of Mother whose mind is liberated from the objects of worldly enjoyment by his desire to live eternally in the peace and bliss of Mother's presence, he is already on a sure way to Libera-tion, as this desire for the proximity of Mother makes the mind rise above other desires. It imparts humility to the devotee's personality, without which no one can bow before the Higher force with any sincerity. It awakens a keen sense of one's incompleteness, which is essential for the attainment of God's grace. For Christ declared:

> Blessed are the poor in spirit, for theirs is the kingdom of heaven.
>
> Blessed are they that mourn, for they shall be comforted.
>
> Blessed are they that hunger and thirst after righteousness, for they shall be filled.
>
> —Matthew 5

This ever-growing "hunger and thirst" to be forever immersed in the blissful peace of Mother's presence is so irresistible that many of the visitors, shunning the luxuries, comforts, and the dignity they had enjoyed hitherto, prefer to take up any task, undergo any hardship, and face any austerity with pleasure, just to be able to live at Jillellamudi. How imperceptibly, but how surely, is one led willingly to the heights of renunciation without even knowing it! This is perhaps what Mother meant when she said:

"States are *given*, not attained,"

or, in reply to the common Telugu proverb that even a mother does not give food if she is not asked:

"Only she is a mother if she can understand the child's need and give even if it does not ask."

On another occasion she said:

"If you become her children, she will give what you need, herself, understanding your need, but if you learn to ask, she bestows only if she is asked!"

The truth of the above statement is borne out in practice by the fact that those who never ask anything of Mother— not even spiritual uplift—but resign themselves totally to her all-protecting grace, are more benefited than the self-righteous and self-styled sadhus who ask for spiritual benefit, more for the vanity of asking for it, or out of ignorance of Mother's ever-protecting grace! Even in the Sastras, *sarana-gati*, or total surrender and resignation, is said to bestow the highest benefit, rather than specific demands made to God. For, the specific demands assist the survival of the ego, which chooses its own demands, whereas total surrender assists its dissolution in the Self.

That she deliberately and actively effects the inner alchemy in us, even when we are far from her, is evident from the assurance Mother had once given to a devotee: "The Mother is always behind you, protecting."

On another occasion she said: "You need come here to see me, but I can see you (wherever you are)."

On yet another occasion she said:

"Mother does not mean the one that is sitting on a cot at Jillellamudi [i.e., her physical body], after all; Mother means the One without the Beginning and the End; the One who is the Beginning and the End."

Compare this with what Lord Krishna said in the *Bhagavad Gita*: "I am the Beginning of all creatures, and I am the End of all."

Why is it that Mother protects us thus by bringing about these inner changes even without our asking her or trying to change ourselves? Did not Mother say, "The phrase 'Mother's protection' is not correct; protection itself is Mother"?

WHEN MOTHER SPEAKS

We often find that when a Self-realised one assumes the attitude of perfect silence, the mind of the devotees is also stilled by an inner alchemy. When we listen to a spirited discourse, our thoughts are stirred by a new force, but rarely do we experience the overcoming of the mind by a stillness when the Wise One speaks. However, this stillness is what we find in the case of Mother. Both when she manifests the depths of Peace which is her nature, and when she utters a crisp reply to a query, the mind of the questioner is suddenly denuded of its narrow bounds that had maintained the turbulence of thoughts and doubts for so long, and the mind is lost in its own infinite expanse.

The technique of breaking down the fossilised forms of misconceptions that fill the common man's mind has been exemplified already by the philosophical observation *neti, neti* (not this, not this). Alan Watts writes in his book *The Way of Zen* that the virtue of the *sunyavada* of Nagarjuna is not to be found in the thought content of his argument. It is only to be valued for the effect of such a method of attack. It demolishes all restrictions of the thinking mind till finally the original nature of Mind manifests itself in their stead. While Nagarjuna employed the method of systematic and patient demolition of every form of thought successively, Mother's cryptic sayings give a paralysing shock to the very quality of the mind's being distorted into petty fixed patterns of ignorance. Not only do her statements accomplish this task at the moment of hearing them, they dig themselves in at the root of the very phenomenon of mechanically accepting systems of thoughts. Whenever these ignorant forms of ideas crop up, the sayings of Mother cause them to short-circuit, as it were, and "break their bones." Her sayings are alive and conscious in this sense. Like them or dislike them, accept them or reject them, but they do their work in your mind all the same. Often this is disconcerting, but there it is.

Discomfited, we are—often unceremoniously, in our efforts to build up pleasant illusions about ourselves and our notions—by the subtle presence of Mother's sayings deep in our mind, nearer to the core of our being. They never allow us to sink into complacency regarding our spiritual state, originality, wisdom, and all other forms of vanity. Reject her words blindly, but soon you will hear the murmurs of your own conscience that you are rejecting your own chances. The more vehemently you criticise them and contradict them, the more deeply you are caught. It is like the soft mud of the village of Jillellamudi. The more you try to pull up one leg, the deeper does the other go down. The more you try not to slip, the more readily you slip. When someone complained to Mother that he slipped in the mud on his way, Mother quipped that the very aim of his journey was to slip into her presence!

Take Mother's definition of *Advaita*, for example:

"It is recognising all as One. The One that is ALL, the One that cannot be comprehended, is *Advaita*."

When someone asked her what she has to say of *Vedanta*, she replied:

"Vedanta is not what can be spoken of; [when discussed] it is what neither the speaker nor the listener understands; in worldly affairs, at least, the speaker knows what he talks about."

Such are her words regarding God:

"He is formless because all forms are His. He is nameless because all names are His."

"He is without attributes because all attributes are His."

Such is her definition of the word Mother:

"The Infinite, Eternal Basis of Existence; the One which is All; the One which has no beginning and no end; the One which is the Beginning and the End."

IN THE PRESENCE OF MOTHER

In the presence of Mother, hours and days trickle by, and one does not feel that he has stayed sufficiently long. The stay at Jillellamudi slowly gets identified in his mind with his very existence. Thoughts rarely rise, and the bliss of thoughtlessness, so greatly praised in books on mysticism, is what one experiences.

However, the reactions of different minds to Mother's presence are as varied as their natural inclinations. A few feel their ego rise up in an attempt to test her wisdom, to "size her up," so to say. Only prolonged experience shows that she assumes the size we assign to her, unless she graces us with a blow to our ego. Others feel intense devotion expressing itself in a feeling that resembles sadness. Yet others feel that she is quite normal, without anything special; such people realise, in the course of time, that this evaluation came from the "thoughtless state" that they had experienced. Of course, absolute thoughtlessness is the fortune of a few. But even the commonest of visitors feels inner peace and contentment swallowing up their world of cares and vexations.

As days pass, the sense of time that makes us cry "we have no time to stand and stare" in our normal world loses its thraldom. It is felt only as a prolongation of one's stay, and not as a force that binds and limits this stay. The whole of one's stay at Jillellamudi is a rarefied experience of time, i.e., time is not experienced as the passage of hours, minutes, and days but as the flux of a "continuous Present Tense," unless one's stay was frittered away in empty conversation with one's companions, or one had been too little attentive to what was happening in the depths of one's mind. Several of those who had complained about their early visits that they had no experience worth the name, in course of time and on careful retrospective introspection came to realize that their self-study was at fault. In fact, I am one such.

"Mother, so many speak about their experiences. Why do I have no experience at all?" I asked her once.

Pat came the reply:

"No experience is an experience in itself."

I was at first dazed.

But today, I can only say that the "no experience" of which I complained is not a continuation of the mental state of our daily lives; on the other hand, it is marked by a lulling of one's mental flagellations. Similar was the answer of Sai Baba of Shirdi to a related question. Even Bhagavan Ramana Maharshi said that visions and such experiences do not necessarily constitute the elevation of the inner spirit to a greater sublimity; the peace that radiates from the silence of the sage is a greater manifestation of inner alchemy in us, according to him. Unconditioned contentment that swallows up all vexations and worries, all worldly attachments, and a perennial flow of inner purity and bliss fill the very core of one's being. This expanse of the self, this flow of purity and bliss, is in itself the goal of all true spiritual endeavour and is felt in Mother's presence even by those who never exerted themselves in that direction.

Those that follow a particular line of sadhana, say mantra japa or nama japa, have experiences of their own, and they are generally of a few types. The more fortunate ones like Sri Yarlagadda Raghavaiah of Singupalem have a mystic darshan of their deity in Mother's form; some find Mother in the picture they worship. Yet others find that, in her presence, sadhana, which they could not carry on with regularity by any amount of effort, goes on of its own accord so incessantly and with such depth that it constitutes their real initiation into it. But the strangest of all is that, some of them, even those who had pursued their sadhana consistently for years earlier, when once they come into her presence, feel that all sadhana is superfluous. They find that even if they break their rigid routine to be in the company of Mother, they are only bettered. A few of them have even given up all sadhana, for they have been fortunate to realize that she took their welfare as her responsibility, leaving nothing to their limited capacities and efforts. In short, those who are already pursuing a line of sadhana find that, in her presence, their effort is widened, deepened, and rendered more all-embracing and unintermittent. In those who never practised any type of spiritual discipline, this profound influence of her presence results in their mind getting more and more centred on Mother—her miraculous form, her incomparable words, and her profound silence. Any habitual fickleness of the mind is checked by the chanting of Mother's name that goes on from the lips of everyone all the time, whatever task they might be physically engaged in at the moment.

Another experience that is usually shared by many people in her presence is that gradually vices and faults in one's personality get rectified. The thraldom of vices is slackened. Excessive irritability, pride, neuroticism, are all gradually eliminated. Sceptics and scoffers of Mother's divinity get gradually transformed, mainly because they find in her the embodiment of the truth of all religions in its pristine, not degenerate, form, which is the result of distortion by ignorant orthodoxy (and of which they had been severe critics). Humility is automatically induced in the heart of the visitor by her august presence—chiefly because he finds in her utter simplicity and perfect wisdom a contrast to his own vanity; and, secondly, because the logic of her words annihilates his egoistic arguments; her questions corner him into a helplessness where he is stripped naked of his illusions of himself. Sometimes her rebuff to the rise of one's vanity is silent and subtle: a proud musician miserably fails, a sadhu who is proud over the camphor or the sugar candy that he can materialise is taught a lesson that this is nothing. The pontiffs run helter skelter under the shower of the hailstones of her questions and replies.

THE INCREDIBLE MOTHER

Every incarnation, while being a manifestation of the eternal and the boundless basis of all existence, is characterised by the camouflage of a common mortal's appearance. Even Lord Krishna, who was described by no less a sage than Vyasa to be the most complete manifestation of Godhead possible in human form, evaded the understanding of all except a few, whom He graced with the sight of His divine form. Even highly evolved souls are characterised by both these qualities, but they attain to it by vigorous effort, whereas incarnations manifest themselves as such. Mother is one such instance.

"I am not anything that you are not, my child," says Mother to the visitor.

"Mine is the state of knowledge–ignorance. I do not know what I know."

But when some of the visitors point to the miracles that they had experienced on account of her grace, she simply says:

"I do nothing. They happen because your faith is great." More convincingly, she adds:

"If I can cure diseases, why should there be any hospitals at all? If I can help the needy, why should so many starve and be poor?"

At another time:

"What a pity! My boy had also failed in his examination,

and my daughter is almost always suffering from a bad headache. I am not able to help my children, dear lady. What can I do for yours?" she replies to a woman who begs for a favour for her son.

Though something within us tells us strongly that she is all-powerful, we are silenced by her misleading logic.

How deceived we are by her words, we come to realize, as we observe her more closely and carefully. As we draw closer to the various inmates of the ashram, everyone comes out with an account of his own experiences and observations that throw a flood of light on what she says. For we come to realize that we are misled by our understanding of her words and that they have a different dimension in their connotations that we can hardly understand, owing to the infinite disparity between her level of being and of our own, if we have being at all. Even these narrations of one's experiences to us does not easily happen. Everyone among them, on being asked for his (or her) experiences by the newcomers, replies that he (or she has none! This should not be taken for a deliberate effort to mislead. For, the same person later gives an account of his experience of his own accord, and his only explanation of this discrepancy will be that Mother's permission was only given then. Indeed, there is a strangeness about the experiences that one has from Mother. Sometimes they get so completely lost from memory that even those who had very remarkable experiences feel that they have none to recount. Sometimes these experiences return to the mind so vividly that it becomes impossible to contain them without expressing them verbally.

Some of these experiences reveal some hidden aspects of this Divine manifestation and open vistas into "the Great Beyond" that is normally concealed from us by the mask of mortality.

One of the strangest and the most enigmatic aspects of Mother is that she never takes any food in a regular way.

"She never knew a morsel of food," her late mother-in-law once sighed, "nor a wink of sleep." Even as a child, I was told that Mother never asked for anything from anybody ... not even food for herself! Even as a baby she never cried for milk. It was left to the late Rangamma to remember the time to give her a feeding. Still she never thinned away or weakened on that account. Mother explained this mystery to some people by saying that she had some ailment that made it impossible for her to eat anything. A blessed "ailment" it is, which very few even among the most rigorous of sages could achieve! She does not even take any substitutes. All that she could be persuaded to take regularly by her devotees is coffee—three or four times in a day, and an ounce or two each time.

Where does she get all the energy and strength, which she sometimes displays, to the utter amazement and shame of even the most athletic of her devotees? That question haunted my mind for quite a long time. But one day I thought I got the clue to this.

A family consisting of the parents and a few children visited Mother and they were beside themselves with joy prostrating to her. Mother said, in the midst of casual talk, that some people are devoted enough to offer first to her whatever they eat, even while staying far away from Jillellamudi. She added:

"But, in their anxiety to hurriedly feed their children with idlis before starting on the journey to Jillellamudi, they offer plain idli to my photo while they dress them with ghee and chutney while eating themselves—and by doing so, they make it difficult for me to eat these idlis."

The couple started shedding tears of joy as they bowed again and again at her feet. Later, I realised that Mother referred only to them all the way through this story. Strange, isn't it?

One Lakshminarayana of Guntur told me of a similar experience that he had. Lakshminarayana and his wife were ardent devotees of Mother. Every day they offered the food that they had cooked before the photo of Mother and partook of it as a gift. Every weekend, when they visited Jillellamudi, Mother used to refer to what was prepared in their house on a particular day, imitating the way they made their offering. She used to tell them when either salt or chillies were used in excess and when they were improperly cooked. When they asked her whether the reference was to them, she replied with feigned anger:

"Do you think that my only business is to see what everyone is doing in his house? Am I a thief? If there is a coincidence between what I said and what had happened in your house, it is only by accident."

But so many and so frequent were these "accidents" that they qualified as what one of our brothers said: "A prefect accident is a miracle."

In the light of such experiences that several others had, I had closely perceived that, even in Jillellamudi, whenever an offering was made in the kitchen room of the free boarding house before Mother's photo, she, sitting on her cot in her thatched hut at a great distance, showed signs of satiation of hunger, of having had a full stomach, and belched.

In view of these incidents, I could dimly perceive the reason behind one of her instructions to the closer devotees: not to beat or drive away creatures like cats, dogs, crows, etc., which might approach the offerings with the intention of eating them when they were being made, but to look upon them as being her own manifestations!

When I once asked Mother whether I should think that she draws her nourishment from what was offered to her by various devotees in various places, she told me that it was not necessary. For the One who is All, and from whom all existence (including the five elements) draws its nourishment, there is no need to draw any nourishment from *anywhere*. That, of course, is her characteristic way of putting things.

Once, some visitors asked Mother:

"Is it true that you have left off food?"

She replied:

"I did not leave food; food has left me."

Those that strive to leave off food would be forced by nature to take to it again and again. It is this inviolable law of Nature to which Mother refers when she says that food had left her. For, the common man is in its grip; it holds him inextricably, whereas Mother was left by it. That is why when she was once asked whether she was not hungry, she replied:

"In this Kali age, there is no hunger for me."

By saying that she did not leave off food, Mother perhaps implied that, for the One who is All beings, there is no question of anything being left off by her.

But those who have the good fortune of being closer to Mother for a long period of time would now and then see that, strangely enough, Mother sometimes orders for something to be cooked specially. Most often, it is intended to be given to someone who, in his mind, perhaps wished to have it, or one whose bad health demanded such food. But, occasionally, she asks as though she wants it herself. Common experience reveals to us that when once we break our abstinence of anything that we had once enjoyed, the habit is revived uncontrollably. And with regard to food, we also find that when we take some extra food on one day, the very next day at the same hour of the day the demand is there again. But in Mother's case it is not so. She asks for food rarely and, again, for *long* periods, she never takes anything, even when she is offered food. Then why does she need that food? What is the underlying mystery? For, we have seen earlier how she could acknowledge all offerings to her by various devotees in various parts of the country.

The close observer of Mother would find that sometimes she is whispering and muttering something as though to herself. But her attention is found to be firmly fixed and directed as though at a person nearby. From her facial features, it can be easily perceived that she is not totally attentive to us. Not that she enters into a trance-like state. For she readily responds to our call, except on rare occasions. One such whispering was the first to raise the curtain over these mysterious requests for food by Mother.

It so happened that, one day in 1964, when all the visitors were sent away to the dining hall, Mother retired to her inner apartment, and only a few of us were sitting there with her. Even while she was talking with us normally, her attention was suddenly and mysteriously diverted, and she no longer seemed to be in our midst mentally. She started saying:

"Syamala, my child, who will look after you? Shall I give you a dosa (pancake) of wheat flour?"

Immediately she broke the thread of her reverie and came into normal awareness. She summoned a lady who was staying there:

"So-and-so is having some wheat flour with her. Make a pancake of it and get it for me."

I was inwardly overjoyed and thrilled at the collaboration of her whispering to us what she was asking for, as though she would really eat it. Who was that blessed lady Syamala? If Mother takes anything, it is clear that it is for some such individual and not for her own sake!

Again, on the 6th of October 1963, a similar incident took place. In the midst of casual talk, Mother suddenly entered the state of a strange other-mindedness and said:

"I had been asking for a pancake for three days. I was not given that so far by the hotel keeper Satyam. Why serve those that are rich enough to have anything they want? Give me that, for I am destitute."

After a little pause, she continued:

"Today I am on a regulated diet. Can you give me two pancakes of wheat flour and some hot water, quickly, in ten minutes?" she asked a lady sitting by her.

Accordingly, everything was prepared and brought. But then Mother refused to take it, saying that just then she had taken barley water. However, on being requested further, she accepted it and started eating it even while lying on her cot. She did not even sit up. While eating, she once again relapsed into "other-mindedness" and said:

"There should be no moisture. Is this improperly baked? If one is not careful, water might accumulate in the womb. Therefore, for today, let there be regulation of diet."

"For whom?" asked one of her closest devotees.

"Do you ask about her?" Mother asked, casting a serious glance at her, and started narrating a story.

But even while she was narrating the story and answering our queries, she was passing once again into that state of "other-mindedness:"

"There is a young lady near Pandharpur, the daughter of a tribal couple. Unable to put up with her domestic troubles, she left for the forest where she is doing penance, that is, meditating incessantly. Someone informed her husband that she had left for the forest. He managed to search her out and behaved rudely towards her. She became pregnant. Her mind is pure even though she is living as a housewife. The child in the womb died. Again, she commenced her penance. She is no longer her former self and is now immersed in penance. Her mother once served in my grandfather's house in Tenali."

Even while narrating this, Mother continued to eat the pancakes in an absent-minded way, and finally, she even put the leaf holding the pancakes into her mouth, being so totally absorbed in attending on that far-off *tapasvini* in the lonely forest. However, one among us hurriedly removed the leaf from her mouth. She then turned to one side and lay quietly. Her prolonged aspect of melancholy and agony on the previous day now assumed a new significance and a new meaning for us on account of what she told us on that day. I felt that the reason for her asking for any eatable has now been revealed to us at least to some extent.

On the 9th of August 1963, when sister Vasundhara entered her house, Mother was taking an oil bath. Mother said to Vasundhara:

"I ate three idlis. They gave me idlis. They gave me idlis nicely dressed in pure ghee!"

"Who gave them, Mother?" asked Vasundhara.

"Someone," she evaded.

"Please tell me," entreated Vasundhara.

"Is there any condition that I must tell you that? Why should I tell you my secrets? Do you tell me yours? I do not tell you." Mother picked up a quarrel.

"Is it Ramakrishna that gave you idlis?"

"He does not offer me."

"Is it brother Seshagiri Rao?"

"No."

"Then please tell me who it is."

"No, I will not."

"A few thousand miles away?"

"No."

"Less than a hundred miles?"

"Yes," replied Mother, as she left the bathroom.

I WILL CONCLUDE THIS subject with an account of my own personal experience. Every year, I celebrate the 19th of August as the date of my first visit to Mother. On that day in 1964, I got payasam (rice boiled with milk and sugar) prepared, and offered it to her after the worship. The payasam was contained in a big vessel that was full, and it was brought straight from the oven; it was extremely hot and steaming. Generally, mother takes just a drop of what is offered into her mouth and returns the rest. On this occasion, she started eating it, in the course of which she entered her state of "other-mindedness." She was eating very hurriedly and, within no time, ate up the whole of it, which is too much even for a good eater. As she ate, her attention was focused on the few inches of space between the cot and the wall, and she went on muttering, "Eat a little more! Just a little, my child," as though she were coaxing a child to eat properly. When all of it was over, she became self-conscious: "Oh, everything is consumed! What do you have for yourself?" she asked me. Before I could say anything, she washed her hands in the empty vessel and said, "You take that!" Her other-mindedness, the absolute impossibility of a single individual eating the whole of it, and the words she was muttering—all were revealing.

Now I know that, if ever she eats anything, or asks for it, it is only for the sake of someone who is either in distress or engaged in *tapas* in some deep forest. Now I understand what she implied in her enigmatic statement that she left half unuttered:

"You can buy and eat anything you want from anyone. But who will look after those who have none to turn to, living in far off forests? Who will look after them?" Now I know who it is that looks after them!

CHAPTER IV

At the Feet of Mother

SRIMATI KRISHNAVENAMMA

AMONG THE INMATES OF the ashram at Jillellamudi, one of the most respected and dearly loved is Krishnavenamma, wife of Sriramulu Venkateswarlu, who is more commonly known as Haridas. How she ever came to know of Mother, and how she was lost in the flood of Mother's grace before she settled permanently in her service, is a subject of deep interest. The whole process of her inward change and experience amply illustrates Mother's statement that "Spiritual states are not achieved but are given."

Krishnavenamma was inherently of a spiritual bent of mind. She worshipped several great saints but derived no tangible benefit besides having a strange dream that often recurred. She used to see and worship in her dreams an acquaintance of hers to whom she was deeply attached. Once she also dreamt that she visited a small village along with her husband. She saw there a freshwater tank having rocky steps, with lotuses and water lilies in it. She also saw a thatched hut in which she saw a housewife who had a big round *kumkum* on her forehead and who was distinguished by her divine features. Krishnavenamma dreamt that they settled in that village.

The morning after her first dream, she described all that she had seen to her husband, who explained to her that the housewife is none other than the Mother of the Universe and that she (Krishnavenamma) is sure to be saved by the Divine in a woman's form. This happened years before they had even heard of the Mother of Jillellamudi.

Years trickled by. They were living in a village called Kakumanu (a few miles from Jillellamudi) when Krishnavenamma was informed that an enlightened lady had come to the adjacent village of Kommur. On the 18th of May 1955, Krishnavenamma visited Mother for the first time and gave her sugar as an offering. Her simplicity and absence of ostentation surprised Krishnavenamma. This marked a turning point in her life. Krishnavenamma, who was distinguished by her unquenchable zeal to visit shrines and holy men in search of grace, after visiting Mother, felt an inner solace and assurance that made further quest superfluous.

Krishnavenamma came to Jillellamudi for the first time in March 1960. She had the urge to touch Mother's feet but it remained unfulfilled. She repeated her visit the following Friday. During both visits, she retired to bed without taking any food at night. Mother sent somebody to find out the reason for her doing so. Krishnavenamma said that she did not feel hungry (a lie), and that she was ready to take her food if Mother prepared and served it. Mother again sent word that tall tales about miracles happening with the grace of Mother were all untrue, and that she need expect no such favours. This did not shake Krishnavenamma's faith. Finally, Mother cooked the food, mixed it herself, and fed Krishnavenamma as a mother does a child. During the conversation, Mother asked her, "Do you have any of your kinsfolk here? Had you ever been to this village earlier?" "By God, no! I never came here earlier," Krishnavenamma said. Mother smiled and turned her face away.

Krishnavenamma reported this to her husband, who was thrilled on hearing Mother's question. He said that Jillellamudi was the village Krishnavenamma had seen in her dream far earlier and that the housewife she saw was Mother. He also told her that Mother's question is a reminder of Krishnavenamma's visit to Jillellamudi in her dream. Krishnavenamma soon remembered that the dream's freshwater tank with little lotuses and the rocky steps, the thatched hut, and the housewife in it all looked the same as those she had seen when she came into the village of Jillellamudi.

Haridas accompanied his wife to Jillellamudi on her second visit. He, too, was caught in the web of Mother's love, and enjoyed the privilege of being personally fed by Mother. He lost himself in joy and loudly recited verses in praise of Goddess Annapurneswari with tears overflowing in his eyes.

The second visit proved a turning point in Krishna-venamma's life. All the experiences that followed paved the way for the permanent settlement of her family at Jillella-mudi. Ever since she returned to Kakumanu, there arose and grew in her an uncontrollable urge to give whatever she had to Mother—ornaments, money, utensils, everything. She went on doing this on every visit. Whether she stayed at Jillellamudi or at Kakumanu, her mind constantly rested at the feet of Mother. Her longing to be in Mother's presence was so intense that the walk of eight miles was nothing for her to undertake once every two days! What fanned her devotion was the extraordinary grace of Mother, for, extraordinary it was. When Krishnavenamma tried to suppress the desire to visit Jillellamudi, Mother used to appear before her physically, laugh at her, approach her, and suddenly vanish before she could muster enough presence of mind either to address her or touch her. Krishnavenamma would immediately start on her walk to Jillellamudi. All the way, she was engaged by Mother with enlightening talk. Krishna-venamma used to see Mother clearly, sitting at Jillellamudi and taking an active part in the conversation across the distance! For Krishnavenamma, her own experience was not a hallucination but a total reality, for, each time, Mother looked the same at Jillellamudi as she appeared to her across the distance, even to the minutest detail of her dress.

Mother appeared to Krishnavenamma in her dreams night after night. Sometimes she seriously discoursed on matters spiritual, and sometimes she played with Krishna-venamma in her dreams. To her utter surprise, whatever Krishnavenamma saw happening in her dreams used to come to pass unfailingly when she visited Mother.

One day, Haridas visited Mother alone. During casual conversation, Mother abruptly asked him:

"If I visit Krishnavenamma now, can she recognise me?"

The shrewd man noted the time when the question was raised. On his return to Kakumanu, he asked his wife as to what had happened to her at that hour. Krishnavenamma told him that while she was lying on a cot, she heard the door being knocked on loudly, but she felt too lazy to open it. The knock was repeated, she told him, but it stopped when she finally wanted to open the door.

On another occasion, Haridas visited Jillellamudi alone. At an odd hour, a young boy of five or six came to his house at Kakumanu. He couldn't talk, and he wore a striped full shirt with folded sleeves. He begged for food by gesture. Krishnavenamma offered to serve him food then and there. But the boy insisted on taking the food with him. When she gave him food, he left the house casting mischievous glances of recognition back at her. She anxiously watched him to see whether he begged at other houses also, as beggars usually do. But the boy walked away. What first raised a strange suspicion in her was the fact that, while he appeared to have gone in one direction to her, to others he appeared to have gone in another direction! When they tried to search him out, he was not to be found anywhere!

Later, when Krishnavenamma visited Jillellamudi, she broached the subject with Mother; but before she had finished her narration, Mother asked her smiling, "Did he not wear a striped full shirt with folded sleeves?" This was a clear proof that she assumed that strange guise herself!

The urge to visit Jillellamudi gradually crystallised into a stern determination to stay at least for one year continuously with Mother. When it seemed impossible in view of domestic responsibilities, Krishnavenamma used to leave her house on the pretext of washing her clothes in the nearby tank, and gave vent to her feelings in an incessant flow of tears and silent prayers to Mother.

During her frequent visits to Jillellamudi, Mother used to detain Krishnavenamma there for a day or two. At night, when she tried to sleep, Krishnavenamma used to experience a strange feeling by which she thought that she was dying. Then Mother would keep Krishnavenamma's head in her lap and hold her pulse in one hand, lulling her to sleep with the other hand. Mother used to recite the divine names of "Hari" and "Rama" till Krishnavenamma fell asleep.

Finally, the awareness of Mother's presence by her side at Kakumanu became uninterrupted. In the early part of the year 1958, Krishnavenamma and Haridas settled in Jillellamudi permanently. After that she dedicated her mind and body to the service of Mother—washing her clothes and giving her the four or five daily baths, each of them demanding nearly fifty to sixty pots of water. These tasks Krishnaven-

amma has been doing alone or with the assistance of someone all these years. Today, she is seen to be intimately moving
with Mother. Whatever her inner development might be, its
outward manifestation is very mysterious. Whenever she
sits and gazes at Mother's form, she soon passes into a trance-
like state wherein her body becomes stiff, her gaze becomes
fixed, and her breath gets almost suspended, and she stays
in that state for hours at a stretch, undisturbed by pinching
or even the blowing of wind against her eyes!

On being asked about her feelings, Krishnavenamma
summed them up in this way: Her earlier thirst to visit
shrines and holy persons is now abated. Her spiritual practices seem out of place amidst the surging tides of Mother's
grace that waft her ahead with no effort on her part. She
said that earlier she had experienced the desire to make offerings like coconuts to Mother, but today she feels that the
money with which a coconut is bought, the mind that impels one to do so, even her soul and body, are already
Mother's by her grace. She offered herself in all entirety to
Mother, and there is nothing that belongs to her to be specially offered to Mother!

R. LAKSHMINARAYANA

Life is so full of events undreamt of that we can never dream confidently of *our* dreams coming true. When they do, we feel it to be extraordinary and uncanny.

The common man cannot dream of coming face to face with a living manifestation of God. Even if he does so in his dream, he realises (later) that this was a turning point in his life.

R. Lakshminarayana (referred to as L. throughout this account), an employee in the Patel Volkart Company, is one such person among the devotees of Mother. Though willing to accept that some sort of an Intelligence lies behind the order in Creation, he was averse to the worship of sadhus, sanyasis, mahatmas, and the like. Even if these existed, L. felt that more harm is done to society by the existence of innumerable "counterfeits." Offering a burning incense stick to the Lord of Dawn was all that he did, most instinctively. Strangely enough, he once dreamt that he was taken to a temple by his aunt and that, when he prostrated at the feet of the Goddess, though only to satisfy his aunt, tears rose in his eyes. The toes of the idol's feet stirred a little when the tears fell over them. Surprised, he looked up at the face of the Goddess. He found a living form there. She patted him gently, saying, "You need not shed tears. I am always there for you."

The dream surprised L. a little and lingered in his mind prominently for some time. Unable to connect it with anything else in his life, however, he forgot all about the dream. But when he did recollect it, the image was vivid, even after a long time. The dream did not at all signify any change in his being, though. He did not seek to make it a reality.

The years rolled by. L. got married and set up his family in Guntur. One day, his aunt Lalithamba visited him on her second trip to Jillellamudi and insisted on his accompanying her. L. was only prepared to permit his wife to accompany his aunt. So Lalithamba and Mrs. L. visited Jillellamudi. Mrs. L. was so impressed with her visit that she soon goaded her husband into going there. One day, when he was feeling sad owing to the break in his personal relationship with his boss, she found him more amenable to her persuasion. So they visited Mother sometime in February 1960. It was a Sunday. A small group of visitors from Chirala was taking leave of Mother. L. found that his mental agony vanished beneath the overwhelming peace of Mother's proximity. All through his stay of two days at Jillellamudi, his mind was centred on Mother. Afterwards L. was irresistibly drawn to Mother every week or fortnight. That it was not a purely subjective feeling was clear to L. from the fact that his highly unbelieving grandmother was soon lost in the surge of deep faith on her very first visit to Mother.

During one Sravanamasa (the month of August), L., accompanied by his wife, visited Mother. He wanted to perform puja to her. In the course of an absorbing discussion with her children, Mother invited L. to sit nearer to her cot. But L. said that he was afraid to do so. "Why should you fear Mother?" asked Mother, and placing one of her feet in his lap, she placed the other near his heart. Henceforth, L. never experienced that sense of fear again in the presence of Mother.

On another occasion, he was persuaded by his friend Kumaraswamy to go to Jillellamudi suddenly. On their arrival, Mother fed them personally and asked them to accompany her to the nearby canal with the rest of her children. At that time L. had not taken his daily bath. So, when a sadhu, who brought with him leaves of the tulasi plant, wanted L. to do the puja as he read out the names of the Goddess, L. at first hesitated. He later realized that Mother was teaching him that it is an inward purity that is more important in the case of devotion to God. It was 8 p.m. by the time they returned from the canal. L. wanted to leave for Guntur. Everyone discouraged him saying that it was too late even to catch the last bus at the seventh-mile bus stop. Then Mother gave him a bunch of grapes saying that by the time he finished eating them, he would get a conveyance. So, on reaching the main road, he ate the rest of the grapes very quickly, hoping thereby to get the conveyance earlier. While he was waiting anxiously to see if Mother's words were going to prove infallible, a lorry came that way and he was given a lift!

Mrs. L. visited Jillellamudi during the early months of her pregnancy and stayed there for several days. L. could not visit her for quite some days. One evening Mother asked her whether she longed to see her husband, and she blushed. Then Mother sent word to L. through Kumaraswamy who was leaving for Guntur that night. But Kumaraswamy forgot to convey the message to L. On Friday, Mr. L. was tossing sleeplessly in his bed thinking about Mother. He suddenly heard a voice say, "Child, come to Jillellamudi on Sunday next!" However, he did not find anyone in the room. Sunday happened to be Christmas day. So he stayed back to greet his boss, a Christian, at midnight, and then started for Jillellamudi by bicycle from Guntur. On the way he slipped and damaged the bicycle. Leaving it at Pedanandipadu, he reached Jillellamudi at 6:30 a.m. on foot.

Mother never allowed Mrs. L. to get up from bed early in the morning, but that morning she woke her up and asked her to get ready to receive her husband. Mrs. L. took it to be a mere joke. But L. arrived at 6:30, too early to have come by bus!

On one of his later visits, L. was held up at Jillellamudi for four or five days by force of events. During this period, he happened to read Mother's conversations with Srimati Rajamma and Kalyanananda Bharati. This marked a major step in the intensification of his awareness of Mother's divinity.

Once Mother asked L. to be present for three days during the ensuing Sankranti. But when the time came for him to visit Jillellamudi in accordance with Mother's words, a notice was issued by his office that no one should leave the place without prior permission. It looked as though this was intended for L., who was known to be visiting Jillellamudi almost every weekend. L. did not want to seek the permission of his boss. "If Mother really wants me to go there, the boss should himself send for me and permit me to go," he said to himself, "or else I shall stay here only, shutting myself up in my house, without taking any food for three days." Before the office was closed for the day, the boss himself sent for him and told him that he could leave if he so wished!

On one of his visits, Mother playfully referred to L. as "the man from Guntakal." L. felt very badly and was on the verge of shedding tears because, if he were transferred to such a distant place, he wouldn't be able to visit Mother so often. He even thought, looking at a dog that passed before him, that the dog was more fortunate than he. Mother noticed his intense feelings and asked him to sit near her. He rested his head on her lap and wept silently. Tears flowed profusely from his eyes and fell on the toes of her feet. The toes stirred a little. He raised his eyes to look at Mother's face. She smiled most benignly and, patting him affectionately, assured him:

"You need not shed tears. I am always there to look after you."

These words struck him in the recesses of his heart. It was a dream that had been realised, and no doubt that it was realised for him by her! The dream that he had years earlier, even before he heard of Mother, had now come to pass!

"I cannot be seen. You see me when I appear to you"— the truth of this saying of Mother was most aptly illustrated to L. He was convinced that years before he had even heard of her, Mother made her grace felt by him.

"Even faith and devotion are what are bestowed by Grace and not what are cultivated," said Mother.

This experience of L. clearly brings out the truth of Mother's statement. He was surprised that the assuring words he heard the goddess say in his dream years earlier were literally the same as those he heard from Mother. The latter were only a confirmation of the former. L. had ample proof that the strange dream he had years before he even heard of Jillellamudi was a green signal to him from Mother, an expression of the fact that she graced him. It only remained to be seen by him whether she looked after his well-being in day-to-day life in all ways. Experiences, however, soon began pouring in to confirm even this point. He came to realise that nothing happened, either in his life or in his family, without her knowledge.

For instance, after the birth of their first daughter, one day Mr. and Mrs. L. argued and quipped about the child resembling one of them. The next week, when they visited Jillellamudi together, they were disappointed to see the very large number of visitors, for they could not have a personal interview with Mother. When they wanted to leave the village along with several others who were seeking Mother's permission to leave, Mother gave *prasadam* to all except these two! She sent word to them and granted them a personal interview. Mrs. L. was holding the newborn daughter in her lap.

"Your daughter resembles your sister-in-law," said Mother gazing at the child.

Mrs. and Mr. L. just smiled in reply. Then Mother admonished them in feigned anger:

"Don't you have anything else to discuss at home?"

IN THOSE DAYS THEY were visiting Mother as frequently as possible—once a week or a fortnight. Whenever they came, she used to refer to the various victuals they had prepared on various days at Guntur, and what was wrong with their preparation and taste! One day she referred to the pancakes that Mrs. L. prepared on a certain day in her home in Guntur:

"The hotel-made pancakes taste better, don't they?" asked Mother, looking intently at the face of L.

Those were precisely the words he uttered days earlier when his wife offered him the pancakes she prepared! Then she turned to Mrs. L. and advised her:

"You are preparing them in a curved pan; they must be roasted on a flat one."

ONE NIGHT, WHEN THEY were together in bed, it occurred to Mr. and Mrs. L. that it was not proper for them to keep Mother's photograph in their bedroom. So they immediately shifted it to the family shrine in the kitchen room. Later, when they visited Mother for the weekend, Mrs. L., without stating what had happened, just said to Mother:

"Pardon us, Mother."

"It's no mistake! It is what is most natural. When you believe that I am omnipresent, what is the need to hide anything from me? There is no need to feel guilty about it," Mother replied.

One day, their daughter Bhagavathi was coughing and weeping all through the night, and she was sleepless. L. took the child in his hands and paced to and fro, singing songs in praise of Mother. At that time, the widowed daughter of his landlady was sleeping in the open air, just near the main gate of the front yard. Suddenly, she heard the words "Do my puja, don't grieve." Immediately, she woke up and saw a middle-aged lady, wearing a white sari with a big kumkum dot on her face, entering through the gate. She walked towards the portion of the house in which L. was living. The landlady's daughter noted that the child suddenly stopped crying. The next day, the landlady's daughter recounted what she saw the previous night, and seeing the photograph of

Mother in L.'s house, identified the mysterious visitor of the previous night to be Mother herself! She then took the photograph and started doing the daily puja to it immediately.

WITH THE PASSING OF time, owing to the pressure of circumstances, it became increasingly difficult for Mr. and Mrs. L. to visit Jillellamudi as frequently as they did. As a result, L. used to lie by the side of his baby at night and, touching her tender feet, would imagine them to be Mother's feet, being satisfied with that. Later, when they visited Mother, she told some visitor about what L. did every day at Guntur. Similarly, she also referred to L.'s habit of taking his child near Mother's photograph and offering her to the photograph to be kissed by it.

ON ONE OF HIS visits to Jillellamudi, L. had the most remarkable of all his experiences. Mother was resting on her cot near the foundations of the temple that is now under construction. There was a small group of visitors sitting around her cot. While all of them were enjoying a chat with her, they were called away for supper. But none of them was willing to leave her bedside. Then, Mother offered to mix the food and feed them all personally. She did so, and when everyone was eagerly awaiting his share to be served, she asked all of them to move to the verandah of the thatched hut. But they were unwilling to do so. The clear sky, the silvery moonlight, the cool breeze, and Mother amidst them was an enchanting scene that they did not want to miss. However, Mother asked them what they would do if it rained. They simply refused to contemplate about something that had no likelihood of happening. Then, putting down the rice, Mother lifted up her hands to the sky and beckoned as she called out: "Come rain, come!" Suddenly, a tiny cloud rushed over their heads and lashed out rain, and they could not avoid running for the verandah to which Mother had directed them earlier!

These and countless other experiences laid the foundations of firm faith in L.'s heart. The commonest of all his experiences, even today, is that, whenever he is a bit sad or depressed, some messenger or message from Mother reaches him. He has forever dedicated himself at her feet!

CHAPTER V

With Her Children

MOTHER FINISHED HER BATH and came and sat on her cot in the hall. One of the ladies among the visitors offered fruits and flowers to Mother, broke a coconut, and lighted camphor before her, sitting quietly for a while. Mother, too, was silent. Then the following conversation took place between them.

Visitor: Mother, I have something to ask of you.

Mother: Tell me, child. But there is nothing that I would do about it.

Visitor: My domestic circumstances are not all right. My daughter-in-law is ailing from a disease.

Mother: I don't know anything about these things, and I don't know what to say. [The visitor expected Mother to foretell her future.]

Visitor: Be gracious, Mother. How can you be ignorant of these things?

Mother: All these (sufferings) are of my grace only.

Visitor: Alas! Alas! Please relieve me of these.

Mother: I shall, when I feel I should.

So saying, Mother retired to her inner apartment.

ONE DAY A VISITOR came to see Mother. He broke a coconut as an offering, but it was found to be rotten. He became very sad and blamed his own sinful nature for the unfortunate incident.

Mother: Give it to me.

Visitor: It is rotten, Mother!

Mother: No, child, your rot is gone!

So saying, she took the coconut and ate a part of it.

Similarly, another visitor offered her an apple he had brought. It was all right to look at. But Mother examined it, said that it was rotten, and forced her finger into it, exposing the rotten portion. The visitor sadly complained: "It always happens so in my case. Perhaps I am all right outwardly and rotten at heart." "No, child," she replied, "I say your rot is gone. I shall take it." Saying this, she ate the rotten portion and proceeded to separate the rot from the rest. "It is not as you said. It is only outwardly rotten. It is sweet at its core," she said, as she exhibited the ripe core of the apple. "You are better than most others," she consoled him.

SOMEONE TOLD MOTHER one day that two orthodox Brahmins who came on that day refused to take water from anyone save a Brahmin. Somebody sitting at Mother's feet said: "You ought to have told them that there are no Brahmins here!"

Mother: Why should you say so? When the appointed time comes, they themselves will change their minds. They must realise it themselves!

ANOTHER TIME, A LADY among the visitors said to Mother:

"Mother, may I ask about something that is weighing on my mind?"

Mother: Yes, you may. But there is nothing that I shall say, and there is no objection just to hear you.

Lady: I have a purpose in my mind. It concerns my husband.

Mother: There is nothing that I can do.

Lady: My husband has been staying away from me for six years. In this matter, I will do as you advise me.

Mother: There is nothing that I can say.

Lady: Please free me from my difficulty, Mother!

Mother: Besides the belief that happiness will come even as suffering has come [for the same reason, i.e., God's will or Time], I know nothing. Just as difficulties have come of their own accord, so will happiness set in.

Lady: We hope that you would solve this problem, Mother!

Mother: I can't do anything.

ON ANOTHER OCCASION A VISITOR wanted her help.

Lady: My mind is disturbed even when I meditate. It has not become stabilised, Mother.

Mother: The unstable (alone) is the mind.

Lady: Some thought or the other rises in my mind.

Mother: That's its nature.

Lady: If we wish to stay here for long, are we to cook for ourselves, or is food provided to us here?

Mother: As you wish. If you are contented to take what you get here, however simple, you may do so. If you prefer to cook for yourselves, you can do so. When the time comes for you to stay here, these doubts do not arise, and simply you happen to stay. When the time comes, you cannot but stay here even if you wish not to, and when the time has not come, you can't stay even if you have come with that intent.

ON THE 1ST OF March 1966 came a brother from Peda Naridipadu. It was his second visit. On his earlier visit, he wanted to ask Mother about several things, but he left without doing so. On this visit he decided to ask.

Visitor: Why do we come and go [i.e., to and from Mother]? I am not able to understand that!

Mother: What have you to say?

Visitor: What is it that we get by seeing you?

Mother: You said that you came to see me! Is not that purpose fulfilled?

Visitor: That's all right. But what do we derive from the visit? This, I could not understand.

Mother: That which had compelled you to come here, and had enabled you to see [Mother] would itself enable you to understand. Whatever is done is done by That only. Whatever we might call it—God, Force, or

Nature—we only do as it impels us. That has impelled you to come here. It has raised this question in you.

Visitor: When do we understand it [i.e., the outcome of the visits to Mother]?

Mother: When the chosen moment arrives! How many years after your birth did your mind turn to this [quest for the Divine]? Since how long did you aspire to come here? Even though you wished to come here immediately [on knowing about Mother], you could not do so. What you aspired for happened at the appointed time. Did you put this question to me immediately on seeing me? No. You are doing so now. There is the passage of time. It is the same even in this case. That which made you come here, That which has induced this insoluble question in your mind, would itself resolve it.

Visitor: Do you mean that there is nothing like my effort?

Mother: If you think you are the doer, then *do it. I* don't dissuade you from it. In my view, there is nothing like your effort. The effort is what is apparent; the impulse (the inspiration or the cause) is incomprehensible. Our legs walk, but the force that makes them walk is incomprehensible. Therefore, we think that our legs are moving. That [illusion] impression is unavoidable. Even though there is nothing like our effort, it appears as though it were there. It is not so to you only; it is the case with all.

Visitor: Do you want me to sit and do nothing, relying on time that does everything at the appointed moment?

Mother: I am not rejecting the one and accepting the other. I only say that even sitting quietly with folded hands does not rest with you. Even though it is evident that there is nothing that is ours, and nothing that we do, That itself would prevent us from sitting quietly and would induce all other actions that we call ours, in us. Even that botheration is God!

Visitor: You mean that Creation itself is God?

Mother: Of course!

Visitor: Do you say that fate or preordination should be accepted?

Mother: It is there, whether we accept it or reject it!

Visitor: What is your opinion regarding disciplines or spiritual endeavours?

Mother: I think that even spiritual endeavour is possible only when That inspires it. You might have read several books and heard several great scholars speak. You might wish to adopt one of the several paths of spiritual discipline meant for you. But you fail to practise it. Why? I don't say that even the failure to practise the same is yours. Even in case you successfully accomplish it, I don't consider it to be your effort. The One that had inspired you to practise is also responsible for your failure to do so. Besides, among the various paths that have been laid down, there is no question of a better or a worse one; whichever path is easy for one to adopt is, I feel, the best one [for him].

Visitor: Then, do you deny the teacher–disciple relationship?

Mother: They say that there are teachers and disciples. How can I deny their existence? But in my opinion, the teacher is not different from God. Only he who can look upon the teacher as God is a true disciple. It is mentioned in the first verse of *The Adoration of the Guru* [*Gurudhyana*] that "the guru is verily Parabrahma." When the teacher is in that state, he is the very manifestation of Godhead. The words that he speaks are themselves mantras, and there is nothing like his initiating [anyone] with a mantra.

The one who just points out the direction to the wayfarer is only a guide but not a teacher. The real teacher alone knows the purpose of a mantra and what mantra is, but he never considers one mantra to be superior to any other, or one teacher to be greater than another.

Visitor: I fail to practise any sadhana, but the restlessness to know something always disturbs me deeply, Mother! [As he said this, tears rose in his eyes.]

Mother: [Passing her hand soothingly on his head] It will reveal itself, child. This urge to know was not there in you from the beginning; it arose only late, though it was not so intense as it is now. A period of time separates these phases. If the time comes for you to know, then it can be known.

The visitor was partly consoled and took leave of her.

ONE DAY A DIVISIONAL engineer who visited Jillellamudi requested Mother to come to his house. Mother replied:

There is no principle as to whether I should or should not visit anyone's house. But it is not possible for me to move to any place. Do not feel that I did not oblige you when you invited me to your place. If the moment [for my visit] comes, I cannot avoid it. That would, of course, be *my* coming, and not your taking me to that place. When it is a question of my coming, then it will not be to your house alone. I wish to visit all my children. Some of you might be well off and have several cars. But there are those who have none of these. Those who cannot afford to offer me a single coconut, they, too, wish that I should visit their houses, as you do. You can come here because you have a car. How can such a poor man come here? Can he invite me? Such people stand out in my view. Even if I do not come to you, you can come to me. As the poor ones cannot come, I have to go to them myself. If I stay in one place constantly, it would be easy for you to see me. Once I had been to the town of Chirala, but a stay of two months was not sufficient to visit all the houses. I could visit only a few!

CHAPTER VI

Sayings

ABOUT HERSELF

I AM NOT THE GUIDE and you are not the wayfarers. I am not the Master and you are not the disciples. I am the Mother and you are the offspring.

Reality itself is my state.

I am the beginning and I am the end.

I am am I.

I cannot be known; you know me only when I make myself known to you.

My state is one of Knowledge-Ignorance.

When I do not discriminate between qualities, where is the discrimination between castes?

I am not anything now that I was not earlier. If there is a difference, it is only in your understanding of me.

I have no *sishyas* [disciples]; all are my *sisus* [children].

Motherhood does not mean mere womanhood. Mother is the Infinite, the Eternal Basis of all existence. It is That which is All, and cannot be understood.

GOD

He who can't be reached even by searching is God.

He is without a name because all names are His. He is formless because all attributes are His. He is free from ideas because Ideation is itself God.

Attachment for some denotes human nature. Attachment for all denotes Godhead.

If Knowledge is Brahman, why not Ignorance?

It is not correct to say *Brahma jnana. Jnana* is itself brahma.

I [manifested] as Thou is Brahman manifested as ego.

I remaining as I is the I-am-the-Brahman state [*Aham Brahmasmi*].

There is no God without Man.

The changing, alone, is the Mind; the unchanging is Divinity itself.

Pain is no pain if it is experienced with joy.

THE WAY

Where is the question of a good way to *Atman*, when everything you see is that?

Not teaching anything is my teaching.

That which is all-pervading is *Atma*. Seeing everything as Atma is *Atma sakshatkara*.

Adopting sanyasa is not right; one should become a *sanyasi*.

Through cognition, cognition should be annihilated.

It is with the mind only that the mind can be cognised.

He who teaches cognition is the Teacher.

Bestowing the nearness of God is initiation.

Experience bestows faith; faith cannot bestow experience.

Only that which dispels all doubt is the real teaching.
Ignorance will be destroyed by ignorance only.

The dualities must be conquered through dualism only.
The Self must be known through the Self only.

Mindfulness is real worship.

Recognising all as One is unification.

Perfect equanimity at all times and in all conditions is *samadhi*.

When righteousness is practised, time itself would liberate you.

The subject of the state after death is irrelevant. If the truth about birth that has already taken place is known, what is to happen will be known.

All creatures—from the smallest to the biggest—are equally capable of Attainment.

The meeting point of "I" and "thou" is the substance and meaning of Brahman.

Practice is possible only when it yields itself to [your] effort.

The Cognition that cognises everything is *hridaya*.

Vedanta is that which is not understood either by the one that expounds it or the one that listens to it.

Volition (*sankalpa*) is bondage. Volition based on duality is human nature. Volition based on unity is divinity.

The appearance of duality is ignorance. All appearing as One is Knowledge.

When the Cognisance that cognises is absent, people cannot recognise even with the help of a lamp.

Mind is itself the *mantra*. Sound is itself the *sacred syllable* [*bija* or *Om*]

Bhakti is childhood. [Karma] yoga is youth. Jnana is old age.

States of consciousness are not *attained;* they occur not only to men but to all creatures. They are only granted.

One may remain in *samsara,* but *samsara* should not be allowed to dwell in one's heart.

Constant awareness is itself worship.

Recognising dualities as *Brahman,* constitutes *Brahamananda.*

Every word becomes a mantra through mindfulness.

Only he who can eat anything is a *bhikshu* [mendicant].

Divinity manifests itself in us as long as we perceive the divinity in others.

Pranayama is breath control, i.e., breath watched through control.

Darkness, which is the basis of light, is the real Light.

Worship is what goes on all the time, not for one day only; nor is it what is merely recited. Continuous awareness is worship.

THE NATURE OF HUMANNESS

If I were to judge people according to their qualities, not one could be allowed to come to me. There is no one who is free from even a single flaw.

The synthesis of the four Vedas is human life.

Disputation with others is a quarrel. Disputation with oneself is yearning.

Experience can lead to theory, but theory cannot lead to experience.

Existence [Being] is itself Space. Now, I am sitting here. This is Space.

Forgetfulness is necessary for man.

DEATH

Forgetfulness is death.

Death is only transformation, not annihilation.

Death is better than a life devoid of suffering.

EFFORT AND CREATION

The will of Nature impels all human effort.

Mind, matter, and the highest goal are all one. What is
it that does not have the highest goal in it? Everything
is of Him. Let anyone precisely say of anything, "*This
is the highest goal!*"

Gradation itself is creation.

The perfection of the sculptor's work is the product of
the blows of his hammer.

As within, so without.

Thoughts arise of their own accord.

Glossary

Abhisheka—bathing of a deity or person in milk, water, or other liquids as an offering

Atma sakshatkara—realizing everything as the Self

Choultry—a lodging house for pilgrims

Cot—a bare bed made of rope or wood

Dhvaja sthambha—flag tower

Gopuram—wedge-shaped South Indian Hindu temple tower

Hridaya—heart

Kumkum—a red powder made from turmeric and slacked lime

Matth—headquarters of an ashram

Muni—a meditating sage

Nishkama karma—selfless work

Padmasana—the sitting lotus pose in yoga

Parnasala—a thatched hut

Pundit—a scholar; one well versed in tradition, ritual, and mythology

Purana—classification of an ancient text in Hinduism; roughly "mythology"

Saddhvi—the female equivalent of *sadhu,* meaning a renunciate

Sambar—a staple South Indian vegetable broth seasoned

with tamarind, mustard seed, curry leaves, asafoetida, urad dal, and other ingredients in various combinations
Sambhavi mudra—the yogic practice of opening the "third eye"
Sankranti—"to go from one place to another place" (to change direction) It also means "one meets another." The time when the sun changes direction mid-winter, giving rise to a major Hindu festival of the same name
Shukla and *Shonita*—Semen and ovum.
Sri—an honorific similar to "Sir" or "Mr."
Srimati—an honorific similar to "Madam" or "Mrs."
Suddha ekadasi—a fasting time determined "pure" by astrological means, as it is uncontaminated by negative influences
Sunyavada—theory of nothingness
Suprabhata—a hymn sung to a deity for awakening him or her early in the morning
Sushumna nadi—in *tantra* and *kundalini* yoga and in many *hatha* yoga schools, the *sushumna* is the key channel within which *shakti* energy (sometimes called the *kundalini* energy) flows
Tapasvini—a female performing *tapas* (austerities)
Taruna—the chosen or the appointed hour (by God).
Vairagya—attitude of turning away from material things
Vidhana—the way or the method
Vidhi—both destiny and duty; also one who ordains
Viraga—see *vairagya*
Viveka—discrimination
Yajnopaveetam—a handmade grass finger ring used in Hindu rituals

About the Author

ACHARYA EKKIRALA BHARADWAJA did his M.A. (English) at Andhra University in 1959, and worked as Lecturer in English in several colleges in Andhra Pradesh from the early 1960s till he quit in the mid-seventies to pursue a spiritual path of life.

Always a seeker of Truth, Bharadwaja visited many saints and religious places in his early years. Jillellamudi Amma, Ramana Maharshi, and Shirdi Sai Baba's lives and teachings made an indelible imprint on his young mind. As a result, he spent a number of years in Jillellamudi, observing and analyzing Amma's philosophy at close quarters.

He authored many books in English and Telugu on Amma, Shirdi Sai Baba, and other saints and godmen. He was also the editor for quite some time of *Matrusri*, the monthly journal in English, published from Jillellamudi by the Publications Division of Sree Viswajanani Parishat there.

Bibliography

ENGLISH

Bharadwaja, Ekkirala. *Life and Teachings of Jillellamudi Amma*. Cochin: Stone Hill Foundation Publishing, 2007.

Bharadwaja, E. *Life and Teachings of Mother*. Jillellamudi: Matrusri Publications Trust (MPT), 1967.

———. *Voice of Mother*. Jillellamudi: MPT.

Bharadwaja, E. and Hemphill, Marva L. (eds). *Glimpse of Mother*. Jillellamudi: MPT.

Dinakar, M. *Ammaness*. Jillellamudi: MPT.

Schiffman, Richard. *Mother of All*. San Diego, CA (USA): Blue Dove Press.

Conway, Timothy. *Women of Power and Grace*. Santa Barbara, CA (USA): The Wake Up Press.

TELUGU

Amma Jeevita Mahodadhi. Hyderabad: Viswajanani Trust.

Chakravarti, A. Kusuma. *Amma Satcharitra* (3 Vols.).

Ashok House No A-45/1 Padda Waltair, Visakha-patnam 530017.

————. *Madhura Smritulu*. Ashok House No A-45/1 Padda Waltair, Visakhapatnam 530017.

————. *Divyaanubhutulu*. Ashok House No A-45/1 Padda Waltair, Visakhapatnam 530017.

Murty, Sripada Gopalakrishna. *Amma Suchinche Kitha Darri* (The New Path Indicated by Amma). Jillella-mudi: MPT.

————. (comp.) *Amma—Amma Vaakyaalu* (Amma—Amma's Sayings). Jillellamudi: MPT.

————. (comp.) *Ammatho Sambhashanalu* (Conversations with Amma). Jillellamudi: MPT.

Prasad, P.S.R. Anjaneya. *Anubhavaala Moota—Amma Maata*. Matrusri Nilayam, 6-2716, Salipeta, 1st St., Arundelpeta, Guntur 522002, A.P.

————. *Ananda Nandanam*. Jillellamudi: MPT.

————. *Matrusree Darpanam*. Jillellamudi: MPT.

Ramakrishna, K. *Hymalayam*. Jillellamudi: MPT.

Rao, Naraparaju Sridhara. *Amma*. Jillellamudi: MPT.

Sarma, Mannava Dattatreya. *Lokabaandhavi*. Jillellamudi, 522113 Guntur Dist., A.P.

Sastry, B.L.S. *Telugulo Mahaavaakyam*. F.F. 889, Manasa Park View, 8-24-6/20821, Subbarao St., Gandhinagar, Kakinada 533004, A.P.

————. *Aksharm Veedhinapadindi.* F.F. 889, Manasa Pak View, 8-24-6/20821, Subbarao St., Gandhinagar, Kakinada 533004, A.P.

————. *Padaarachana.* F.F. 889, Manasa Park View, 8-24-6/20821, Subbarao St., Gandhinagar, Kakinada 533004, A.P.

Sastry, L.S.R. Krishna. *Aksharaanjali: A Compilation of Poetry.* Jillellamudi: MPT.

'Seshu'. Raagabandham, Free Verses. Jillellamudi: MPT.

Vasundhara, Brahmandam. *Srivaari Charanasannidhi* (From the Diaries of Brahmandam Vasundhara). Jillellamudi: Amma Prachuranalu.

————. *Mahopadesam* (A book containing conversation between Amma and saint Rajamma). Jillellamudi: Amma Prachuranalu.

Other Books from Stone Hill Foundation Publishing

Timothy Conway, Ph.D.
WOMEN OF POWER AND GRACE

Jillellamudi Amma (Anasuya Devi) is one of the nine extraordinary, feminine expressions of the Divine vividly portrayed in this highly-acclaimed, eye-opening book chronicling the stories of some of the greatest and most radical holy women of the modern era, from Hinduism, Christianity, and Islam. Here are their deeply moving stories, filled with awesome virtues and compassionate miracles. The section on Mata Amritanandamayi ("Amma," the "hugging saint" of Kerala) is considered the best condensed account of her life and words available in print. Dr. Conway's deep understanding of the teachings of all traditions is infused with a vital devotional or *bhakti* component that is not frequently found in such accounts written by academicians. The result is a book that is accurate, exciting, inspiring, and obviously relevant to all readers. *Includes 5 Indian mystics, 120 pages of quoted teachings, and 40 photos.* **352 pp., Rs. 650 (ISBN 81-89658-26-3)**

Swami Siddheswarananda
THE METAPHYSICAL INTUITION: SEEING GOD WITH OPEN EYES

These unusual and moving commentaries on chosen verses of the *Bhagavad Gita* masterfully unlock the sacred text's mystical insights in an uncommon way. These are the last writings of the extraordinary Swami Siddheswarananda, who was born into the royal family of Cochin, Kerala, India, and became a monk of the Ramakrishna order. He spent most of his life, however, in service to French adherents of Vedanta. He founded and, until his death, was the spiritual head of the *Centre Vedantique Ramakrichna* in the picturesque river town of Gertz, France. This book is the culmination of a lifetime of spiritual search and includes commentaries on aspects of the *Mandukya Upanishad*.

In these teachings, the Swami seeks to convey an experience of an intuition operating beyond logic, outside the play of opposites, through which seekers can more readily sense the nature of reality. To elucidate his meanings and to make them broadly accessible, the Swami draws on the writings of others including Meister Eckhart, Ramana Maharshi, Adi Sankara, Hubert Benoit, and Sri Ramakrishna and Swami Vivekananda. **180 pp., Rs. 295 (ISBN 81-89658-01-8 Editions India; ISBN 0-97-49359-8-0 Arunachala Press)**

Isaac Shapiro
ESCAPING FROM A DREAM TIGER

Another of the author's spirited and direct challenges to the status quo of the mind, dramatically presented in dialogues from his meetings: "Peace is what is found when our mind stops. It becomes quiet, and that is why we come together." As seekers share their questions with a self-realized teacher, we can't help but see the folly of personalizing our usual concerns. When others ask the very questions on our own minds, it becomes obvious that we all have the same mental mechanisms. This book offers an opportunity to really see who is shaping things, who is thinking our thoughts, who is breathing our bodies. Observing this is the highest quest. "It's not casual. It has to consume you," Shapiro cautions. **176 pp., Rs. 275 (ISBN 81-89658-03-4)**

Isaac Shapiro
IT HAPPENS BY ITSELF: DIALOGUES WITH ISAAC SHAPIRO

A dialogue with a self-realized teacher is an opportunity to be yourself as never before, an encouragement to experience life directly, a call to let go of your false identity. This is an invitation to come to the end of "good" and "bad," and see beyond the whole movie. If you have good and bad, there will be fear. To come to the end of this is to really see who you are. Isaac Shapiro is one of those rare human beings who have the courage to walk their talk. Urged by his teacher, H.W.L. Poonja (known as Papaji), he guides seekers from all parts of the world, gently, with compassion and humor, away from suffering and confusion to the very heart of their being, to freedom, to That which is. And how does all this happen? Shapiro indicates quite convincingly that it happens by itself. **176 pp., Rs. 275 (ISBN 81-89658-02-6)**

Alan Sasha Lithman
AN EVOLUTIONARY AGENDA FOR THE THIRD MILLENNIUM: A PRIMER FOR THE MUTATION OF CONSCIOUSNESS

Described by the controversial American priest and theologian Matthew Fox as "a radical book, a compassionate book, and an altogether needed book," this is a call for all of us to evolutionary activism. (It was first published with support from the Institute of Noetic Sciences.) Lithman spent 21 years (1969–1990) in Auroville, the pioneering global community experiment south of Chennai where he apprenticed in "applied spirituality," multicultural community-building, and hands-on environmental restoration. The thrust of his evolutionary agenda, inspired by the evolutionary vision of Sri Aurobindo, is to shift us as a species from a transcendence-based approach to spirituality and problem-solving to a transformation-oriented evolution of consciousness, bridging the egoic schism between matter and spirit. Readers will be given an entirely new way of looking at the meaning behind our evolutionary crises as well as positive steps to more consciously address them, opening the door to our future possibilities as an ongoing species. **248 pp., Rs. 350 (ISBN 81-89658-19-0)**

Steven Harrison
THE QUESTIONS TO LIFE'S ANSWERS

This book gives access to the alternatives to lives of stress and separation in a direct, informal approach, beginning with the unsatisfactory answers we've accepted to our dilemmas and finding out what the real questions should have been. In this original and inspiring work, Steven Harrison lays bare the workings of the mind with brilliant clarity. Grappling with the questions we all have about life, he deconstructs the prevailing spiritual, therapeutic, and self-help methods we use to try to change ourselves. By taking this journey of exploration with him, we come face to face with the unknown and the potential for radical transformation.
184 pp., Rs. 275 (ISBN 81-89658-17-4)

Steven Harrison
WHAT'S NEXT AFTER NOW?: POST-SPIRITUALITY AND THE CREATIVE LIFE

The author, whose seminal work *Doing Nothing: Coming to the End of the Spiritual Search*, helped guide spiritual seekers to the experience of the present without practices, now takes us one step further into the transforming experience of a "post-spiritual" life. Spiritual seekers by the thousands have come to the end of the masters and gurus, the religions and philosophies, and the process of "getting better." The spiritual marketplace has discovered the "power of now" and learned all about the present moment—but is that it? Is it that simple? What's next after now? When we give up spirituality—not out of a reaction or because we have completed some mythical journey—and we drop into the present, what is the post-spiritual reality and how do we live it creatively? Steven Harrison probes these questions, deepening the discovery that the present is a place of boundless creativity in which we can be constantly challenged and inspired to fulfill the wonders of the human potential. Steven Harrison is one of the most insightful and provocative authors in the arena of spiritual inquiry today. **160 pp., Rs. 250 (ISBN: 81-89658-11-5)**

Steven Harrison
BEING ONE: FINDING OUR SELF IN RELATIONSHIP

"The mind cannot be happy," notes Steven Harrison. Circumstances won't bring lasting happiness, not even the cave of the recluse. The mind is the wrong go-between, also, to help us with our relationships.

Then? "Then" is what this book is about, as this best-selling author looks at the possibilities for peace and pleasantness in close relationships between people who remain confused and conflicted despite having found companionship and love. Are humans suitable companions for one another, even after graduating from all the one-on-ones and workshops on self-fixing?

Well, maybe, he says, if they are so fed up that they give up. Thoroughly exhausted from trying to bring about the myth, they can finally experience what extraordinary changes are possible when self-centered effort no longer blocks free-flowing life in all its originality. **160 pp., Rs. 225 (ISBN: 81-89658-16-6)**

Sankara Saranam

GOD WITHOUT RELIGION: QUESTIONING CENTURIES OF ACCEPTED TRUTHS

Multi-Award-Winning Book and Recipient of the USABookNews.Com Best Books Spirituality Award

Preface By Arun Gandhi

Using time-tested tools of spiritual investigation, it becomes possible to examine our present beliefs, explore the nature of God and sense of self, and ultimately expand our identity. This book introduces this age-old approach to spiritual inquiry for modern-day readers. Step by step, it offers a bridge between organized religion and mystical spirituality for anyone questioning traditional dogma or its legacy of divisiveness. It also assists in overcoming limitations and notions of exclusivity promoted by New Age movements. Included are 17 universal techniques for developing a personal relationship with God and broadening our view of ourselves, others, and all of life. **336 pp., Rs. 475 (ISBN 81-89658-09-3)**

Madhukar

THE SIMPLEST WAY

Madhukar's teaching is so relaxed that he encourages people not even to relax. Relaxing is too much effort, he says. In the dialogues of this spiritual teacher it is obvious that he is not willing to settle for anything less than what already exists, which he calls our True Being, the Essence. Why this is not an actuality to most is pursued by him through the tangle of concepts and words we call our lives. Identifying ourselves with our moods, positive and negative opinions, the poison that is our doubts, and the tyrants called feelings are some of the aspects he identifies as the ego-centered programming of many lifetimes. With his guru H.W.L. Poonja, affectionately called Papaji, this former TV broadcaster in Germany became immersed in effortlessness, and he is now effectively communicating this ease in meetings in the West and in India. **Editions India 256 pp., Rs. 325 (ISBN 81-89658-04-2) International edition available under the Arunachala Press imprint.**

Eli Jaxon-Bear

THE ENNEAGRAM OF LIBERATION: FROM FIXATION TO FREEDOM

Eli Jaxon-Bear presents a radically new model for moving beyond the ego and the psyche, a fresh approach to awakening through the use of the ancient Enneagram's nine fixated structures of ego to clearly describe who you are NOT. There is a living intelligence in all people that seeks ultimately to discover its true identity and source, says Eli. In the light of direct self-inquiry, limitations that once seemed to define oneself are discovered to exist only on the surface of consciousness in one's imagination. The author shows how to look into the wisdom mirror of the Enneagram to see past all false identification to the truth of being. **276 pp., Rs. 395 (ISBN 81-89658-00-X)**

Rupert Sheldrake
A NEW SCIENCE OF LIFE

Why do many phenomena defy the explanation of conventional biology and physics? For instance, when laboratory rats in one place have learned how to navigate a new maze, why do rats elsewhere seem to learn it more easily? Rupert Sheldrake describes this process as *morphic resonance*: the past forms and behaviors of organisms, he argues, influence organisms in the present through direct connections across time and space.

The first edition of this book created a furor when it appeared, provoking the outrage of the old-guard scientific community and the approbation of the new. The British journal *Nature* called it "The best candidate for burning there has been for many years." A lively debate ensued, as researchers devised experiments testing Sheldrake's hypothesis, including some involving millions of people through the medium of television. These developments are recorded in this revised and expanded edition.

Rupert Sheldrake, Ph.D., is a former Research Fellow of the Royal Society, a scholar of Clare College, Cambridge, and a Frank Knox Fellow at Harvard University. Currently, he is Perrott-Warrick Scholar in Psychical Research, Trinity College, Cambridge University. **272 pp., Rs. 450 (ISBN 81-89658-20-4)**

Rupert Sheldrake
THE PRESENCE OF THE PAST

The author's theory of morphic resonance challenges the fundamental assumptions of modern science. An accomplished biologist, Rupert Sheldrake proposes that all natural systems, from crystals to human society, inherit a collective memory that influences their form and behavior. Rather than being ruled by fixed laws, nature is essentially habitual.

This book lays out the evidence of Sheldrake's controversial theory, exploring its implications in the fields of biology, physics, psychology, and sociology. At the same time, Sheldrake delivers a stinging critique of conventional scientific thinking, which sees nature as a machine that, although constant and governed by eternal laws, is nonetheless somehow evolutionary. In place of the mechanistic, neo-Darwinian worldview, he offers a new understanding of life, matter, and mind. **394 pp., Rs. 650 (ISBN 81-89658-21-2)**

Rupert Sheldrake
THE REBIRTH OF NATURE

One of the world's foremost biologists, Rupert Sheldrake has revolutionized scientific thinking with his vision of a living, developing universe with its own inherent memory. In this book he urges us to move beyond the centuries-old mechanistic view of nature, explaining in lucid terms why we can no longer regard the world as inanimate and purposeless. Through an astute critique of the dominant scientific paradigm, Sheldrake shows how recent developments in science itself have brought us to the threshold of a new synthesis in which traditional wisdom, intuitive experience, and scientific insight can be mutually enriching. **260 pp., Rs. 450** (ISBN 81-89658-22-0)

Michael Murphy
THE LIFE WE ARE GIVEN

George Leonard, a founder of the "human potential movement" in the West, together with another internationally known pioneer of personal growth programs, Michael Murphy of California's world-famous Esalen Institute, developed this guide for those who want access to the most effective life-changing practices. Together they outline an extraordinarily practical route to physical and spiritual enrichment that all can follow for a lifetime of deeply satisfying personal growth. "*The Life We Are Given* is a synthesis and culmination of seventy years combined experience by two of the wisest and most pioneering explorers and teachers of the possibilities of human transformation. I recommend it highly."—Dean Ornish, M.D., president and director, Preventive Medicine Research Institute. **210 pp., Rs. 350 (ISBN 81-89658-43-3)**

Stone Hill Foundation Publishing Pvt. Ltd.
G-309, Panampilly Avenue
Panampilly Nagar
Cochin 682 036
Kerala, India

By phone: 0484-232-1513 or 0484-401-2517
By email: stonehillfoundation@asianetindia.com
By fax: 0484-232-1778